To Ms Nancy Iliff
from
Lu

BABALU!

Favorite Recipes from Top Latin Chefs and Celebrities of the Latin World

by Michael Valdes and Art Torres

GPG

GENERAL PUBLISHING GROUP

LOS ANGELES

Publisher: W. Quay Hays
Editorial Director: Peter L. Hoffman
Editor: Dana Stibor
Art Director: Susan Anson
Production Director: Trudihope Schlomowitz
Prepress Manager: Bill Castillo
Production Artist: Bill Neary
Production Assistants: Tom Archibeque, David Chadderdon, Russel Lockwood
Copy Editor (English): Dianne Woo
Translators: Martha Corona, Minerva Figueroa
Food Photographer: Butch Monserrat
Front Cover Logo: Annie Sperling-Cesano

For information:
General Publishing Group, Inc.
2701 Ocean Park Boulevard, Suite 140
Santa Monica, CA 90405

Library of Congress Cataloging-in-Publication Data
Valdes, Michael.
    Babalu! : favorite recipes from the world's top Latin chefs
and celebrities / by Michael Valdes and Art Torres.
      p.   cm.
    ISBN 1-57544-031-8 (hardcover)
    1. Cookery, Latin American.   I. Torres, Art. II. Title.
TX716.A1V26 1998
  641.598—dc21
                                    98-22762
                                      CIP

Printed in the USA by RR Donnelley & Sons Company
10 9 8 7 6 5 4 3 2 1

General Publishing Group
Los Angeles

CONTENTS

ACKNOWLEDGMENTS

There are a great many people without whose undying help and encouragement this project could not have reached fruition. First and foremost, our deepest gratitude and thanks to the celebrities and chefs who took part in *Babalu!* We have admired your talent and we thank you for your generosity in sharing your culinary talents to help fight breast cancer.

To our good friends and publishers, Quay and Sharon Hays, our editors, Peter Hoffman and Dana Stibor, our art director, Susan Anson, and the complete staff at General Publishing Group; food photographer Felipe "Butch" Monserrat; and food expert Orlando Ramirez. A very special acknowledgment to Amy Langer, executive director of the National Alliance of Breast Cancer Organizations, for her dedication and tireless efforts.

Also, to the following people who played a role in seeing this work to its present form: Alexandra Alvarez, Liza Anderson, Rosanne Atencio, Jeanne Barnaby, Celia Becquer, Mario Beguiristain, Odisa Beltran, Tony Cabral, Betty Cortina, Stephanie Dark, Audrey Davis, Lori De Waal, Dena Du Bouf, Twyla Duncan, Rose Fahey, Becky Fajardo, Minerva Figueroa, Carmen Fumero, Janice Garcia, Michael Goldsmith, Dr. Leonard Gordon, Martha Gutierrez, Mike Hernandez Sr., Kim Jakwertz, Becca Kovacik, Fernan Martinez, Paula Murphy, Al Nodal, Steven Noriega, Bernie O'Connor, Constanza Oranja, Luis Penalas, Omer Perdillo, Steve Roseberry, Michel Ruben, Ignacio Saralegui, Laurie Ann Schag, Maribel Schumacher, Nancy Seltzer, Mily Soberon, Carmen Suarez, Mark Teitelbaum, Karen Tencer, Tina Thor, Elisabeth Valdez, Senator John Vasconcellos, Jerry Velasco, Cindy Villareal, Jerry Vukas, Aury Wallington, Dick Weaver, and our parents.

Even with this extensive list, we are certain to have forgotten others who played a role in *Babalu!* To those, our apologies and our gratitude.

FOREWORD

As Latinos, we have always been proud of the richness of our culture, our language, and our cuisine. The language that binds us and the commitment to family is also a thoroughfare through our lives. To know us is to know the wonderful secrets you will be given throughout this culinary journey.

The recipes in this book are given with love from the hearts and souls of some of our most gifted talent. We present them with pride as a testament to who we are in the Americas and beyond.

There is another purpose to our journey: to educate Americans about breast cancer. We have chosen to donate a percentage of the proceeds raised by this book to the National Alliance of Breast Cancer Organizations (NABCO). We have selected them as our beneficiary because of their tireless work and outreach capabilities across the nation. They also publish their information in Spanish, thus reaching a segment of our population not normally targeted for this education.

On a personal note, one of us is the son of a breast cancer survivor, and we know that this disease can strike anyone. We also know that faith and the support of one's family can dramatically increase the chances of survival! Art's mother, a woman of tremendous strength and faith, has proven this to us and his family. It is for that reason that we have chosen to dedicate this book to Julia Torres and all the other breast cancer survivors who persevere.

ART TORRES AND MICHAEL VALDES
APRIL 1998

INTRODUCTION

If I had to group together the individual cuisines of the South and Central American countries under the heading of "Latin cookery" and define it with just one phrase, it would be "of the earth." For thousands of years, the people of these countries have relied on the bounty of the land to provide life, shelter, and, most of all, nourishment. The land continues to be worked and harvested by proud, hardworking people who love and care for the soil in the hopes that it will give life back to them. It is truly a circle of life.

In Latin American homes, the mothers and grandmothers give of themselves in the meals they prepare—it is a way to love. Today's Latin dishes have evolved in home kitchens, changing from village to village, region to region. Although the foods of Latin America's many countries have several common elements, I see the cuisine not as a melting pot, but more like a woven basket: The strands—the ingredients, cooking techniques, and cultures—are woven together but retain their own unique identities.

Above its surface, the soil yields essential Latin foods such as corn, tomatoes, plantains, rice, a variety of beans, wheat for flour, fresh herbs, and numerous chilies. Below its surface grow potatoes, onions, peanuts, and indigenous roots such as yuca, jicama, and camote that are key ingredients in Latin cooking. And no Latin kitchen is complete without luscious cheeses such as Idiazabal, Manchego, and Cotija. Columbus' discovery of the New World and its many culinary treasures more than 500 years ago transformed and continues to transform the food cultures of the world. Potatoes, tomatoes, corn, chilies, peanuts, chocolate, and sesame seeds are only a handful of the riches introduced to the world from the Americas.

At my restaurants in Houston, we pay homage to the ingredients that we as a continent have provided the world and to our role in changing the way the world eats. We also wish to express that in South America, we didn't just replace the indigenous cuisines with the Europeans' as was done in the North, but merged them to create wonderful new flavors. I believe that all food should be "yummy." In my travels, I have come across chefs who are so concerned with being exotic and unique that they have left all pleasure out of the formula. Latin American cooking can be as exotic and unique as one wants it to be without losing this key element.

I think authentic Latin cuisine is simple and unpretentious—peasant food of sorts—and very earthy in texture, appearance, and often taste. Examples include moles, sopas, foods smoked with corn husks, and stews. The flavors are sometimes brightened with lime and other fresh citrus, avocado, refreshing cilantro, and tropical fruits. Today's chefs do not always prepare authentic Latin American dishes, but they capture the essence of the foods of their homelands and re-create them with contemporary imagination.

The following pages contain special recipes contributed by a select group of well-known Latinos. These are dishes that they have created or that have been passed down to them. The chefs and celebrities have each contributed to this admirable, noteworthy project to help in the fight against breast cancer. We represent a wide cross section of Latin countries, and just as in our everyday lives and our particular careers, these foods represent our homelands, our heritage, and our pride in being Latino. We hope you find pleasure in preparing these recipes for and with your family and friends. *Provecho!*

MICHAEL J. CORDUA
MAY 1998
OWNER/CHEF, AMERICAS & CHURRASCOS RESTAURANTS
HOUSTON, TEXAS

INTRODUCTION

There are approximately 30 million Latinos residing in the United States, and their cultural influence has become a staple in our society. Who can imagine visiting Los Angeles without being able to find a good Mexican restaurant? Or New York without its rich Puerto Rican influence?

Babalu! is a special project because it demonstrates the unity, while celebrating the diversity, that exists among all of our subcultures that are bonded by a common language. Cubans, Mexicans, Spaniards, Puerto Ricans, and all other nationalities are called to the table in harmony to eat pierna, enchiladas, paella, and picadillo, and we extend that invitation to those open to discovery and those willing to embrace the warmth of our people. For those of us who had to leave our homelands because of political, religious, or personal reasons, a safe haven is provided here by keeping the integrity of our cuisine—our heritage—intact.

The second reason *Babalu!* is so important is the fact that it benefits the National Alliance of Breast Cancer Organizations, the leading nonprofit central information resource on breast cancer and a network of more than 375 breast cancer organizations nationwide. It is also one of the largest outreach providers to the Spanish-speaking community. We lose about 45,000 women every year from this disease. This is an alarming figure that becomes personal when you realize it can strike your wife, mother, daughter, or friend. As a general rule, Latin women are not educated about breast cancer because of a cultural stigma that exists with a woman's body. These myths need to be dispelled to save countless women from this tragic illness.

I want to express my thanks to you for purchasing this book, and I hope you enjoy the journey you embark upon between its covers.

EDWARD JAMES OLMOS
MAY 1998

NABCO
NATIONAL ALLIANCE
OF BREAST CANCER
ORGANIZATIONS

ABOUT NABCO

The National Alliance of Breast Cancer Organizations (NABCO), based in New York City, is the leading non-profit information and education resource on breast cancer with a network of 375 member organizations.

Through publications, on the phone, and on the Internet, NABCO's Information Services staff offers information and resources to medical professionals and their organizations; women at risk; patients and survivors and their families; government and voluntary agencies; and the media. With public and corporate partners, NABCO's education and outreach programs have been successful in bringing women the facts about the disease and connecting them with needed services.

NABCO also plays a leadership role as an advocate for the needs and concerns of the general public, women with breast cancer, and the underserved in national and local legislative and regulatory decision making.

INFORMATION ABOUT BREAST CANCER FROM NABCO

Breast cancer is the most common form of cancer in women in America, with more than 180,000 cases diagnosed each year. Although the means for its prevention are not yet known, finding the disease early offers the best chance to treat it successfully. With early detection and prompt, state-of-the-art treatment, 97 percent of breast cancer patients are alive five years after diagnosis. There are two million breast cancer survivors in the United States today.

EACH WOMAN SHOULD HAVE HER OWN BREAST HEALTH PROGRAM THAT INCLUDES:

- A healthy lifestyle, including regular exercise and a low-fat diet to maintain a slim weight. Don't smoke, and use alcohol in moderation, if at all. Research shows that this healthy behavior may decrease breast cancer risk.

- Regular mammograms (breast X-rays) every year, starting at age 40. Mammograms are safe and can be obtained at one of more than 5,000 facilities that are now certified and inspected by the U.S. government.

- A breast examination by a doctor or nurse every year, starting at age 20. Clinical breast exams are a complement to regular mammograms, which together find small breast cancers at their earliest stage.

- Regular breast self-examination. Each woman should become familiar with her breasts and what feels normal for her. Anything unusual or persistent should be checked by a health professional.

- Knowing your family's health history and discussing it with your doctor. A family history of breast or ovarian cancer—especially in a mother, sister, or daughter—may mean a different personal health plan.

A number of national organizations offer free information about breast cancer, including reading material and other resources; referral to breast cancer risk, screening, and treatment experts; special awareness events; and sources for financial assistance and emotional support. If we can help you or someone you know, contact NABCO toll free at (888) 80-NABCO, or on the Internet at www.nabco.org.

ALBÓNDIGAS AL "SON SABOR" (CUBAN-STYLE MEATBALLS)

½ yellow onion, chopped
6 cloves garlic, finely chopped
½ red bell pepper, chopped
¼ cup dry wine
1 tablespoon white vinegar
2 tablespoons salt
1 tablespoon sugar

½ pound ground beef
1 whole egg
1 cup flour
½ cup bread crumbs
¼ cup oil
1 can tomato sauce

Separate out half of the onion, garlic, bell pepper, dry wine, vinegar, salt, and sugar for the sauce.

Mix the ground beef with the remaining onion, garlic, bell pepper, dry wine, vinegar, salt, and sugar. Knead the meat with all the above ingredients. Add the egg and flour and knead again. Finally, add the bread crumbs and knead again.

In a deep skillet, heat the oil. From the reserved ingredients for the sauce, add the onion, garlic, and bell pepper, sauté lightly, and add the dry wine, vinegar, sugar, and salt. Stir for 30 seconds and add the tomato sauce. Cover at low heat.

Take small portions of the meat and form into balls. Cook in the sauce for 20 minutes.

Serve hot, preferably with white rice, green salad, and plátanos.

SERVES 4

½ cebolla amarilla, picadita
6 dientes de ajo, bien machacados
½ ají rojo, picado finamente
¼ taza de vino seco
1 cucharada de vinagre blanco
2 cucharadas de sal
1 cucharada de azúcar

225 gramos de carne molida (picadillo res)
1 huevo
1 taza de harina
½ taza de pan rayado
¼ taza aceite
1 lata de salsa de tomate

Separar la mitad de la cebolla, ajo, ajies, vino seco, vinagre, sal, y azúcar para la salsa.

Poner la carne molida con el resto de la cebolla, ajos, ajies, vino seco, vinagre, sal, y azúcar. Mezclar todo, amasar la carne con todos los ingredientes. Añadir el huevo, la harina, y amasar de nuevo. Finalmente, agregar el pan rayado y amasar.

Poner en un sartén hondo el aceite con la cebolla, ajos, y ajies. Freir ligeramente, agregar el vinagre, vino seco, azúcar, y la sal. Moverlo por 30 segundos y agregar la salsa de tomate. Dejarlo tapado a fuego lento.

Tomar la masa y con una cuchara sacar porciones pequeñas. Redondearlas en la palma de la mano. Cuando toda la masa este hecha bolitas, póngalas una por una, tápelas por 20 minutos.

Se sirven calientes, y de preferencia acompañadas con arroz blanco, ensalada verde y plátanos maduros.

SIRVE 4

FLAN DEL CONSUELO (FLAN FOR CONSOLATION)

4 cups milk
1 can sweetened condensed milk
1 cinnamon stick
2-inch piece of lemon peel
2 cups sugar (divided use)
1 teaspoon vanilla
5 eggs

FOR THE SAUCE:
½ pound strawberries or raspberries

The easiest way to make this dessert is to use a special flan mold with a lid and cook it for 15 minutes in a pressure cooker, but I am assuming you don't have either of those. You can also make it in the oven. In a saucepan, boil the milk and the condensed milk, the cinnamon stick, and the lemon peel for a couple of minutes. Allow to cool while you prepare the rest. Heat the oven to 300 degrees.

To make the caramel, melt 1½ cups of sugar with two tablespoons of water in a small saucepan. Boil, stirring occasionally, until it has a dark honey color, but don't let it burn. Put the mixture in a Pyrex glass baking dish. Tilt the dish from side to side to spread the caramel evenly on the bottom.

To make the flan, remove the cinnamon stick and the lemon peel from the milk. Add the vanilla and eggs, slightly beaten. Pour into the Pyrex dish and bake in the oven for an hour. To avoid burning the flan, place in a larger pan filled halfway with water to steam the pudding.

To prepare the sauce, mash the berries with a fork and add the remaining sugar. Let rest until the sugar dissolves. It is not necessary to cook it, but you can speed the process by boiling it for a minute. Allow to cool.

Serve the flan cold with the berry sauce. Enjoy!

SERVES 8

Isabel Allende

MY RELATIONSHIP WITH MY MOTHER IS BASED ON COMPLICITY, IRONY, AND MUTUAL MEMORIES. SHE IS MY EDITOR, THE ONLY PERSON WHO CORRECTS MY MANUSCRIPTS BEFORE THEY ARE PUBLISHED. WE ARE UNITED BY MANY THINGS, NOT ONLY SENTIMENTS AND LITERATURE. COOKING IS ONE OF THEM. I HAVE KNOWN THIS WOMAN, MY MOTHER, FOR MORE THAN 50 YEARS, AND I HAVE NEVER SEEN HER SERVING THE SAME DISH TWICE. SHE ALWAYS MAKES CHANGES AND DECORATES HER FOOD WITH ORIGINALITY: IN HER HANDS A CABBAGE BECOMES A WORK OF ART. ONE OF THE FEW RECIPES THAT NEVER CHANGES IS HER FLAN DEL CONSUELO, WHICH WOULD TRANSLATE ROUGHLY AS FLAN FOR CONSOLATION. IT GOT ITS NAME FROM THE FACT THAT MY MOTHER USED TO PREPARE IT EVERY TIME WE HAD TO GO TO THE DENTIST, GET A SHOT, OR OTHERWISE FACE ANY OF THE MULTIPLE TERRORS OF CHILDHOOD. FOR MY BIRTHDAY, INSTEAD OF THE USUAL CAKE, SHE WOULD MAKE ME THIS

FLAN DEL CONSUELO

1 litro leche
1 lata leche condensada azucarada
1 palo de canela
1 trozo cáscara de limón
2 tazas azúcar
1 chucharadita esencia de vainilla
5 huevos

POR LA SALSA:
225 gramos fresas o frambuesas

En casa de mi madre este postre se prepara en una flanera con tapa, que se coloca dentro de una olla a presión y se hace hervir por 15 minutos, pero como supongo que usted no cuenta con ninguna de las cosas, le explicaré cómo hacerlo en el horno. Ponga a hervir la leche con la leche condensada azucarada, la canela, y la cáscara de limón durante un minuto. Retire del fuego y deje enfriar un poco. Mientras tanto encienda el horno a 300 grados.

Prepare en una ollita o un sartén el caramelo con una taza y media de azúcar y 2 cucharadas de agua, hirviéndolo hasta que tome un color dorado obscuro, pero sin quemarlo porque se pone amargo. Vierta de inmediato el caramelo en un pyrex (recipiente refractario) y muévalo para cubrir el fondo.

Ahora haga el flan. Retire la canela y la cáscara de limón de la leche tibia. Agregue a la leche la vainilla y los huevos ligeramente batidos (clara y yemas juntas). Vierta en el pyrex acaramelado y hornee por una hora. Para que no se queme, el pyrex debe ponerse al horno sobre una bandeja o recipiente con un poco de agua.

Prepare la salsa para decorar machacando con un tenedor las fresas o frambuesas y agregando la media taza de azúcar que sobró. Deje reposar hasta que se deshaga el azúcar y póngala en la nevera. No es necesario hervirla.

Se sirve frío acompañado con la salsa de fruta. ¡Qué lo disfrute!

SIRVE 8

Isabel Allende

DESSERT. ON THOSE SPECIAL OCCASIONS, IT CAME WITH WHIPPED CREAM AND HOT CHOCOLATE SYRUP INSTEAD OF THE USUAL BERRY SAUCE. THE COMBINATION OF FLAN, CARAMEL, CHOCOLATE, AND CREAM CAN INDUCE A SAINT TO COMMIT AT LEAST ONE OF THE DEADLY SINS: GLUTTONY. I DON'T KNOW HOW MANY CALORIES THIS FLAN HAS, BUT I ASSUME IT MUST BE AROUND HALF A MILLION...

PISTO MANCHEGO

2 onions
4 tomatoes
4 green pimientos*
Olive oil
Salt

Peel the onions, pimientos, and tomatoes, discarding the seeds. Cut into quarters. Heat the oil in a saucepan over medium heat. Add the onions and cook until brown (about 4 to 5 minutes). Add the tomatoes and the pimientos. Cook for 15 minutes, stirring occasionally so that the mixture doesn't stick to the bottom of the pan.

Ideally served with fried eggs, roast pork, or as a bread topping.

*Pimientos are large, sweet red peppers. The green variety may be hard to find fresh. Green bell peppers may be substituted, but they are not nearly as sweet or succulent.

SERVES 2

---

2 cebollas
4 tomates
4 pimientos verdes
Aceite de oliva
Sal

Pelar las cebollas, los pimientos, y los tomates, quitando las semillas. Después cortar en cuadritos, todo ello por separado. Poner el aceite en una sartén y a fuego medio calentar. Añadir la cebolla y dejarla hacer 4 o 5 minutos. Agregar el tomate y el pimiento, sazonar y dejar cocer todo junto durante 15 minutos a fuego medio. Mover de vez en cuando para que no se pegue al fondo de la sartén.

Es ideal para acompañar huevos fritos, carne de cerdo frita, o para tomar sobre el pan.

SIRVE 2

PASTEL PUDIN DE PLÁTANO (BANANA PUDDING CAKE)

3 eggs
1 cup oil (any kind, canola is what I use)
3 very ripe bananas
2 cups flour
1 cup sugar
2 tablespoons cinnamon
⅓ cup chopped walnuts
1 tablespoon baking powder

Preheat oven to 350 degrees. Mix the eggs, oil, and bananas in a blender, then pour the mixture into a bowl and add the rest of the ingredients. Place this mixture in a Pyrex loaf pan. Place the pan in the oven for 45 minutes or until the cake is golden brown.

MAKES 1 LOAF

---

3 huevos
1 taza aciete (cualquier tipo, yo uso canola)
3 plátanos muy maduros
2 taza harina
1 taza azúcar
2 cucharadas canela
⅓ taza nueces, cortadas
1 cucharada polvo para hornear

Encienda el horno a 350 grados F. Mezcla los huevos, aceite y plátanos en una batidora. Luego mezcla todo con los ingredientes que quedan. Póngalo en un plato Pyrex (refractario resistente al calor.) Ponga el Pyrex en el horno y hornéelo por 45 minutos hasta que quede dorado.

HACE 1 PASTEL

Maria Conchita Alonso

MY GRANDMOTHER, THEN LATER MY MOTHER, USED TO MAKE THIS DISH ON SPECIAL OCCASIONS. TO ME, THIS DISH REPRESENTS FAMILY. IT HAS BEEN IN OUR FAMILY FOR GENERATIONS, AND WE STILL LOVE IT.

I HOPE YOU WILL LOVE IT TOO!

Lucie Arnaz

ARNAZ PICADILLO (A KIND OF CUBAN HASH)

1 medium onion
1 medium green bell pepper
4 cloves garlic (Arnazes never count, we go by the mood we're in)
3 small potatoes
1 large egg, hard-boiled
½ cup canned baby peas
2 large pimientos
¼ cup vegetable oil
¼ cup Spanish olive oil

1½ pounds ground beef
½ cup canned crushed tomatoes (fresh would be terrific, just peel them or substitute tomato sauce)
¼ cup dry sherry
1 tablespoon salt
1 tablespoon Worcestershire sauce
½ teaspoon Tabasco sauce
¼ cup dark raisins
Salt and black pepper

Chop the onion, seed and chop the bell pepper, mince the garlic, peel the potatoes and chop into ¼-inch pieces, chop the egg, drain the peas, and chop the pimientos.

Heat the vegetable oil in a medium-sized skillet over medium heat and toss in the chopped potatoes. Fry until crispy brown (10 to 12 minutes). Set pan aside.

In a large, deep skillet or casserole pot, heat the olive oil over low heat until it begins to smell fantastic. Add the garlic and onion and stir it up a bit. Then add the bell pepper. Stir over low heat for 8 to 12 minutes (or until tender). Add ground beef and stir until it browns (maybe 10 minutes).

Add the tomatoes and any juices, sherry, salt, Worcestershire sauce, and Tabasco. Stir over medium heat 15 to 20 minutes. No need to cover.

Toss in the potatoes and raisins. Add salt and pepper to taste and cook until the liquid is absorbed (maybe another 10 minutes).

When it's ready, serve on a large platter. We like to use a huge round earthenware plate that my stepmother, Edie, used to serve Dad's on. Make a small hole in the center and sprinkle the chopped egg into it. Decorate the outer rim with the peas and lay the pimiento pieces wherever they make you happy.

If you serve this with a traditional avocado and red onion salad (dressed with a little Spanish olive oil and just a smidgen of balsamic vinegar), you'll be in Havana hash heaven.

SERVES 6 TO 8

ARNAZ PICADILLO

1 cebolla mediana
1 ají verde, mediano (pimiento verde)
4 dientes de ajo (los Arnaz nunca
    cuentan, vamos con lo que sentimos
    en el momento)
3 papas pequeñas
1 huevo, hervido y bien cocido
½ taza guisante pequeño enlatados
2 pimientos largos
¼ taza aceite grandes vegetal
¼ taza aceite de oliva Español

680 gramos carne de res (picadillo)
½ taza lata de tomates, machacados
    (o use frescos, o puede sustituir salsa
    de tomate)
¼ taza jerez seco
1 cucharada sal
1 cucharada salsa Worcestershire
½ cucharita Tabasco
¼ taza pasas obscuras
Sal y pimienta

Pique la cebolla, quite la semilla, y pique el ají, corte el ajo, pele las papas, y córtelo en pedazos de ⅗ centímetro. Ponga a hervir el huevo y córtelo. Colar los guisantes y cortar los pimientos.

Ponga a calentar el aceite en un sartén mediano sobre fuego medio y ponga las papas a freír hasta que estén hechas (10 a 12 minutos). Ponga el sartén a un lado.

En otro sartén hondo, ponga a calentar el aceite de oliva sobre fuego lento hasta que dé un aroma fabuloso. Añadir el ajo y cebollas y revolver un poco. Luego añadir el ají. Revolver sobre fuego lento por 8 a 10 minutos. Añadir la carne de res y revolver hasta que esté cocida (casi 10 minutos).

Añadir los tomates y los jugos, jerez seco, sal, salsa Worcestershire y tabasco. Revolver sobre fuego medio por 15 a 20 minutos sin cubrir.

Añadir las papas y pasas. Cocinar hasta que el líquido esté evaporado (otros 10 minutos).

Cuando esté listo, sírvalo en un recipiente grande. Nosotros tenemos uno en la cual, mi madrasta, Edie, le servía a mi padre y es la que a nosotros nos gusta usar. Haga un pequeño hoyo en el centro y ponga el huevo, hervirdo y partido. Decore alrededor con los guisantes y ponga las rajas de pimiento donde guste.

Sírvalo acompañado de una ensalada tradicional de aguacate y cebolla roja (con un poco de aceite de oliva Español y vinagre balsámico) y te encontrarás en el cielo de picadillo de Habana.

SIRVE 6 A 8

SOMETIMES IT TASTED BETTER.

I MARVELED AT THE WAY HE COULD "SMELL" THINGS TOGETHER. ANYWAY, THIS RECIPE IS MINE, NOT DAD'S, CULLED FROM TRIAL AND ERROR—TRYING TO FIGURE OUT HOW HE DID IT AND NOT BEING SATISFIED UNTIL IT CONJURED UP THOROUGHBRED HORSES, SUNSETS AT THE BEACH, IMPORTED MARIACHIS, JIMMY DURANTE AT THE PIANO, AND MY FATHER SERENADING US AFTER DESSERT AMID CIGAR SMOKE AND COGNAC.

IT WAS THE BEST OF TIMES!

CRISPY RISOTTO CAKE WITH ROASTED CORN AND CRABMEAT WITH AN HERB SALAD

FOR THE RISOTTO CAKE:
1 white onion, diced
1 tablespoon olive oil
1 pound Arborio rice (risotto)
1½ cup white wine

1½ quart water
1 tablespoon Italian parsley, chopped
3 tablespoon Parmesan cheese, ground

Sauté in a medium skillet over medium heat the diced white onions in the olive oil until just translucent. Add the Arborio risotto to the onions and toast for approximately 2 minutes. Add the white wine and reduce until dry, stirring all the while. Add the water in three parts, stirring constantly, making sure the liquid is absorbed before adding the next part of water. Cook the risotto until al dente and pour into a baking pan. Cool. Season risotto with the parsley and Parmesan cheese, mixing thoroughly so the parsley is evenly distributed. Shape into perfect disks about 1½ inches square.

FOR THE CORN AND CRABMEAT RAGOUT:
3 ears fresh corn
2 tomatoes, diced
16 ounces corn broth
1 tablespoon chives, chopped

3 red onions, grilled and chopped
1 pound crabmeat
1 ounce butter

Using a sharp knife, trim the ends of the corn cobs so they stand flat. Then, pushing down with the knife, strip the kernels from the ears of corn. Place in a baking dish and roast in a 350-degree oven for 10 minutes. Meanwhile, cut the cobs in half and place in a saucepan with 20 ounces of water. Bring to a boil and simmer for an hour until all the milk is released from the corn cobs. Strain and reserve for later. Meanwhile, mince chives and dice onions. Pick through crabmeat, making sure all the shells are removed.

In a small sauté pan over medium heat, combine all ingredients for the corn and crabmeat ragout and cook until heated through.

FOR THE HERB SALAD:
2 tablespoons parsley sprigs
1 tablespoon bronze fennel sprigs
1 tablespoon dill sprigs
1 tablespoon garlic chives

2 handfuls baby arugula, washed
½ tablespoon tarragon, picked
1 tablespoon olive oil
1 tablespoon shallots, diced

Combine parsley, fennel, dill, chives, arugula, and tarragon in a stainless-steel mixing bowl. Lightly wilt the herb salad with olive oil and diced shallots.

To assemble the dish, spoon the ragout into the center of a large serving dish. Sauté the risotto cake in an oiled skillet over high heat until crispy and hot and place on top of ragout. Delicately place the wilted herb salad onto the risotto cake.

SERVES 10

Octavio Becerra

OCTAVIO BECERRA WAS PLANNING A CAREER AS A COMMERCIAL PHOTOGRA-PHER WHEN HE HAPPENED TO OBSERVE GUEST CHEF JOACHIM SPLICHAL PRE-PARE TWO SPECIAL MENUS FOR THE RESTAURANT WHERE OCTAVIO WAS WORKING AT THE TIME. HE WAS HOOKED. NOW, 12 YEARS LATER, HE HAS BEEN NOMINATED FOR "RISING CHEF STAR OF THE YEAR" BY THE JAMES BEARD FOUN-DATION FOR HIS CULINARY TALENTS AT L.A.'S PINOT BISTRO, AND WAS MADE PARTNER, ON HIS 30TH BIRTHDAY, AT PINOT BISTRO BY HIS MENTOR, JOACHIM SPLICHAL.

IN 1983, OCTAVIO APPRENTICED WITH SPLICHAL AT MAX AU TRIANGLE IN BEV-ERLY HILLS. HE WORKED HARD AND QUICKLY ROSE TO THE POSITION OF SOUS CHEF. AFTER MAX AU TRIANGLE, SPLICHAL ARRANGED FOR OCTAVIO TO WORK IN EUROPE AT TWO- AND THREE-STAR MICHELIN RESTAURANTS, MOST NOTABLY AZARK IN SAN SEBASTIAN, SPAIN, AND AT THE ONE-STAR LEONCE IN

FLORENSAC IN THE SOUTH OF FRANCE. THERE HE IMMERSED HIMSELF IN ALL ASPECTS OF THE CUISINE, INCLUDING THE SEASONAL GROWING AND DAILY CHOOSING OF INGREDIENTS. "IT'S NOT JUST LEARNING A NEW LANGUAGE," OCTAVIO SAYS, "BUT LEARNING TO WRITE POETRY IN THAT LANGUAGE."

UPON HIS RETURN TO THE UNITED STATES, OCTAVIO BEGAN TRAVELING ALL OVER THE COUNTRY WITH SPLICHAL, HELPING TO IMPLEMENT THE MANAGEMENT AND FOOD PREPARATION TRAINING PROGRAMS SPLICHAL DESIGNED FOR VARIOUS HOTEL AND RESTAURANT PROJECTS. THE WORK TOOK THEM ON A LEARNING EXPERIENCE THROUGH AUGUSTA, GA., CHICAGO, ILL., ASPEN, COLO., AND THE FLORIDA KEYS. THEIR CHALLENGE WAS TO DEVELOP CUSTOMIZED FOOD CONCEPTS FOR EACH INDIVIDUAL ENVIRONMENT.

IN 1991, TWO YEARS AFTER PATINA RESTAURANT OPENED, OCTAVIO BECAME ITS CHEF DE CUISINE. DURING THAT TIME, HE BEGAN PLANNING WITH SPLICHAL THE CREATION OF PINOT BISTRO. OCTAVIO HAS ALSO CONTRIBUTED TO THE LAUNCH OF THE OTHER PINOT RESTAURANTS.

TORTITAS CRUJIENTES DE ARROZ CON MAÍZ ASADO Y CANGREJO CON ENSALADA DE HIERBAS

PARA LAS TORTITAS DE ARROZ:

1 cebolla blanca, cortada
1 cucharada aceite de oliva
450 gramos arroz (risotto) Arborio
1½ taza vino blanco

1 litro agua
1 cucharada perejil Italiano, cortado
3 cucharadas queso Parmesano, rallado

Freír las cebollas en el aceite de oliva en un sartén mediano a fuego medio hasta que estén transparentes. Agregue el arroz a las cebollas y tuéstelo por 2 minutos. Agregue el vino blanco y reduzca hasta que esté seco, moviéndolo todo al rato. Agregue el agua en tres partes, moviendo constantemente, y asegurándose de que se absorba el líquido antes de añadir le siguiente cantidad de aqua. Cocine el arroz hasta que esté "al dente" y póngalo en una cacerola para hornear. Déjelo enfriar. Sazone el arroz con el perejil y queso Parmesano, asegurándose de mezclarlo bien para que el perejil esté bien distribuído, y fórmelo en discos perfectos de más o menos 3½ centímetros.

PARA LA MASA DE MAÍZ Y CANGREJO:

3 mazorcas frescos, asado
2 tomates, cortados
450 gramos caldo de maiz
1 cucharada cebollitas verdes

3 cebollas rojas, asadas
450 gramos cangejo
30 gramos mantequilla

Usando un cuchillo afilado, corte las puntas de las mazorcas para que puedan quedarse sin moverse. Después, presionando hacia abajo con el cuchillo, quite los granos de la mazorca. Póngalos en un plato para hornear y áselos por 10 minutos en un horno de 350 grados. Mientras tanto, corte las mazorcas (sin los granos) a la mitad y póngalas en una olla con 568 gramos de aqua. Cuando llegue a hervir, déjelo hervir a fuego lento por una hora hasta que las mazorcas hayan soltado toda la leche, cuele y guarde el líquido para más tarde.

En un sartén pequeño a fuego medio, combine todos los ingredientes para la masa de maíz y póngalos en el centro de un cuenco grande para pasta.

PARA LA ENSALADA DE HIERBAS:

2 cucharada perejil
1 cucharada hinojo bronce
1 cucharada eneldo
1 cucharada tallos de ajo

2 manos lechuga arugula, lavada
½ cucharada estragón, fresco
1 cucharada aceite de oliva
1 cucharada cebollita sverdes, cortado

En un cuenco para mezclar, deje macerar ligeramente la ensalada de hierbas con el aceite de oliva y la cebollita picada.

Para preparada el platillo, ponga un poco de la masa en el centro de un plato (para servir). Saltée la tortita de arroz en un sartén engrasado a fuego alto hasta que esté crujiente y caliente. Póngalo encima de la masa. Con cuidado ponga la ensalada de hierbas sobre la tortita de arroz.

SIRVE 10

SALMON WITH APPLEWOOD SMOKED BACON, GARLIC, AND HORSERADISH POTATOES

10 ounces Applewood smoked bacon, diced
5 ounces garlic, blanched and sliced thin
1½ tablespoons olive oil
½ teaspoon cracked black pepper
1 tablespoon Italian parsley, chopped
3 pounds Atlantic salmon filet
1 wooden plank, preferably oakwood (soak for 30 minutes to 1 hour before using)

40 fingerling potatoes, roasted until golden
26 green onions, grilled and chopped
1 teaspoon prepared horseradish
½ pound baby arugula
1 teaspoon balsamic vinegar essence

Cook bacon until crisp, dispose of rendered fat, and set aside. In a large bowl, combine the bacon, garlic, olive oil, pepper, and parsley. Cover the salmon with the mixture to create a crust. Place the salmon on the wooden plank and bake at 350 degrees for approximately 20 to 25 minutes. While the salmon is cooking, toss the potatoes with the green onions, horseradish, and arugula.

Place the potato mixture in the center of a dinner plate and the baked salmon on top of the potatoes. Garnish with a drizzle of the balsamic vinegar essence over the salmon.

SERVES 10

SALMON CON TOCINO AHUMADO, PAPAS CON AJO Y RABANO PICANTE

280 gramos tocino humado Applewood picado
140 gramos ajo, cortado fino
1½ cucharada aceite de oliva
½ cucharita pimienta negra
1 cucharada perejil Italiano, picado
1½ kilogramos filet de salmón Atlántico
1 tabla de madera, preferiblemente roble (poner en remojo durante 30 minutos a 1 hora antes de usar)

40 papa chiquitas, asada hasta dorado
26 cebollas verdes, asada y cortada
1 cucharita rabano picante, preparado
500 gramos lechuga arugula
1 cucharada esencia de vinagre balsamico

Cocine el tocino hasta que esté crujiente, guarde la grasa a un lado. En un recipiente grande combine el tocino, ajo, aceite, pimienta y perejil. Cubra el salmón con la mezcla para crear una corteza. Ponga el salmón sobre la tabla de madera y hornéelo a 350 grados por 20 a 25 minutos. Mientras el salmón se está cociendo, mezcle las papas con las cebollas verdes, rabanos picantes y arugula.

Ponga la mezcla de la papa en el centro de un plato para servir y ponga el salmón encima de las papas. Adorne el salmón con el vinagre.

SIRVE 10

WARM CHOCOLATE TART WITH COFFEE NOUGATINE SAUCE

FOR THE CHOCOLATE TART:

½ cup brewed espresso
1¼ cups unsalted butter
6 ounces bittersweet baking chocolate, chopped

½ cup sugar
6 egg yolks
6 egg whites
½ cup pastry flour

Preheat the oven to 350 degrees. Heat the espresso and butter in a small saucepan and add the chocolate. As the chocolate melts, stir to incorporate all ingredients. In a bowl, whip ¼ cup of the sugar with the egg yolks until firm ribbon forms. In another bowl, whip the remaining ¼ cup sugar with the egg whites to form a light meringue. Combine these three mixtures with the pastry flour. Transfer the batter to a 9-inch cake pan 2 inches deep. Bake for 15 to 20 minutes or until tart rises. Remove from oven and allow to cool. Return to oven and bake again until exterior becomes firm but tart is still moist inside.

FOR THE CREME ANGLAISE:

1 quart milk
1 vanilla bean, seeds only (split pod and scrape)
16 egg yolks
1¼ cups sugar

In a heavy-bottomed pot, scald the milk and vanilla bean seeds. Set aside. In a bowl, combine the egg yolks and sugar. Slowly add some of the milk-vanilla mixture to temper the eggs. Pour the eggs into the milk mixture. Stir continuously over medium heat until mixture thickens. Remove from heat and let cool.

FOR THE NOUGATINE SAUCE:

2 cups powdered sugar, plus 5 ounces
3 ounces almonds, coarsely ground
3½ ounces coffee beans, ground
Creme Anglaise (from preceding recipe)

In a high-sided saucepan, add the sugar and a teaspoon or more of water. Stir until sugar begins to caramelize and turns medium brown. Add the almonds and coffee and stir until smooth. Cook 2 minutes over low heat. Pour out onto a stainless-steel or marble counter or a stainless-steel baking sheet (coated with nonstick cooking spray) and spread as smooth and thin as possible. Allow to cool, then break into small pieces. Grind in a food processor until fine. Pass results through very fine strainer. Reserve pieces too coarse to go through for use as garnish.

Mix coffee nougatine powder with all of the Creme Anglaise in a proportion of 3 tablespoons of powder for each cup of Creme Anglaise. Allow to infuse for at least 1 hour.

FOR THE KUMQUAT COMPOTE:
½ cup granulated sugar
¼ cup water
45 kumquats, cut and seeded
15 mint sprigs, julienned

In a heavy saucepan, stir sugar over heat until it dissolves and turns pale brown. Slowly add water. Bring to a boil and simmer for 5 minutes. Place kumquats into this simple sugar syrup. Cool, then add mint.

FOR THE GARNISH:
½ pint heavy cream, whipped
Coarse coffee nougatine pieces

Slice chocolate tart into small wedges, then heat and place on plates. Pour about 2 tablespoons of coffee nougatine sauce on each. Garnish with whipped cream and coarse pieces of nougatine left from the grinding. Spoon sauce around. Garnish with a spoonful of kumquat compote.

SERVES 15

TARTA TEMPLADA DE CHOCOLATE CON SALSA DE CAFÉ

½ taza café espresso
1¼ tazas mantequilla sin sal
160 gramos chocolate, picado
½ taza azúcar

6 yemas de huevo
6 claras de huevo
½ taza harina de pastel

Precaliente el horno a 350 grados. Caliente el café y la mantequilla en un sartén pequeño y viértalo sobre el chocolate. Mientras el chocolate se derrite, incorpore todos los ingredientes. En un recipiente bata ¼ de taza de azúcar con las claras de huevo para formar un merengue ligero. Combine estas tres mezclas con el harina. Transfiera la masa a un recipiente para hornear que sea de 5 centímetros de profundidad. Hornee por 15 a 20 minutos o hasta que la tarta se esponje. Saque del horno y déjela enfriar. Métala al horno y horneela nuevamente hasta que el exterior esté firme, pero jugosa por dentro.

PARA LA CREMA ANGLAISE:
1 litro leche
1 semilla de vainilla

16 yemas de huevo
1¼ tazas azúcar

En una olla de fondo grueso, caliente la leche y las semillas de vainilla. Póngala a un lado. En un recipiente, combine las yemas de huevo y el azúcar. Agregue un poco de la mezcla de la leche y vainilla lentamente a los huevos. Vierta los huevos a la olla que contiene la leche. Mueva continuamente a fuego medio hasta que espese. Retire del fuego y deje enfriar.

PARA LA SALSA NOUGATINE:
2 tazas azúcar glas, mas 140 gramos
90 gramos almendras, molidas
100 gramos granos de café, molido
Crema Anglaise (de receta dada)

En una olla (de orillas altas) agregue el azúcar y una cucharadita de agua. Mueva hasta que el azúcar empiece a caramelizarse y sea de un color marrón. Agregue las almendras y el café y mueva hasta que esté sin grumos. Cocine por 2 minutos a fuego lento. Viértalo sobre una superficie de acero inoxidable (cubierta de aceite o mantequilla) o de mármol y extiéndalo hasta que quede lo más delgado posible. Déjelo enfriar, y rómpalo en trozos pequeños. Tritúrelo en un procesador de alimentos hasta quedar muy fino. Páselo por un cernidor. Guarde las piezas que sean muy grandes para la decoración.

Mezcle el polvo de nougatine con toda la Crema Anglaise con una proporción de 3 cucharadas de polvo por cada taza de Crema Anglaise. Déjelo macerar por una hora, mínimo.

PARA EL COMPOTE:
½ taza azúcar granulada
¼ taza agua
45 kumquats, picados
15 hojas hierbabuena, picada

En un sartén revuelva el azúcar hasta que se disuelva y esté de un color marrón claro. Lentamente agregue el agua. Cuando hierva, déjelo hervir a fuego lento por 5 minutos. Ponga los kumquats en este jarabe de azúcar. Enfríe y agregue la hierbabuena.

PARA LA DECORACIÓN:
½ taza crema
Pedazos de nogatino de café grandes

Divida la tarta de chocolate en trozos triangulares pequeños. Después caliente la tarta de chocolate y póngala en platos. Ponga más o menos 2 cucharadas de salsa sobre cada una. Decore con crema batida y los trozos grandes del nougatine. Ponga la salsa alrededor. Decore con una cucharada del compote.

SIRVE 15

PAN DE MAMA (MAMA'S HOMEMADE BREAD)

4 cups flour
1 packet Fleischman's yeast
½ teaspoon salt
½ cup sugar
2 eggs

1 stick (¼ pound) butter or margarine,
  melted
¾ cup warm milk
¾ cup water
1 cup dark (not golden) raisins (optional)

In a large bowl, mix the flour, yeast, salt, and sugar. Add the eggs and butter. Mix well. Add the milk, then the water, while mixing ingredients. Add raisins, if using. Mix well by kneading into doughy consistency. After kneading the dough, cover the bowl and let stand until dough rises to double its size (approximately 2 to 3 hours).

Remove cover and punch dough down to remove air bubbles. Divide into pieces to fill desired containers halfway. Roll out the divided pieces to remove any additional air bubbles. Shape as desired into containers and cover. Let stand to rise again, approximately 2 hours. Preheat oven to 350 degrees.

Place in oven and bake for 35 to 45 minutes or until golden brown. Remove bread and brush lightly with butter, if desired.

MAKES 1 DOZEN ROLLS

---

4 tazas harina
1 paquete levadura Fleischman's
½ cucharita sal
½ taza azúcar
2 huevos

114 gramos mantequilla o margarina,
  derretida
¾ taza leche tibia
¾ taza agua
1 taza pasas obscuras (opcional)

En una cazuela grande, mezcla la harina, levadura, sal, y azúcar. Añadir los huevos y mantequilla derretida. Mezclar bien. Añadir la leche, y luego el agua en lo que se continúa mezclando. Añadir las pasas. Mezclar y amasar en una consistencia de masa. Después de amasar la masa, tapa la cazuela y deja que la masa crezca a un tamaño doble (2 a 3 horas).

Destápalo y dale golpes a la masa para remover las burbujas de aire. Divídelo en pedazos para llenar los deseados recipientes a la mitad. Aplastar la masa dividida para remover las burbujas de aire de nuevo. Tapar de nuevo y deje crecer otras 2 horas. Encender el horno a 350 grados.

Póngalo en el horno por 35 a 45 minutos o hasta que asté dorado. Sacar del horno y cepillar con mantequilla, si lo desea.

HACE 1 DOCENA

Benjamin Bratt

IN MY CHILDHOOD, THE SWEET SMELL OF THESE FRESH-BAKED LOAVES WOULD WAKE MY SIBLINGS AND ME IN THE EARLY MORNING. SITTING IN THE KITCHEN WITH OUR MOTHER, WE'D BREAK OFF BIG WARM HUNKS OF THIS BREAD AND SMOTHER THEM IN BUTTER AND JAM, THEN DIP THEM INTO HOT CUPS OF *CAFÉ CON LECHE* OR *CHOCO-LATE*. THE BEST!

FRICASE DE POLLO (CHICKEN FRICASSEE)

½ medium onion, chopped
1 green bell pepper, chopped
1 red bell pepper, chopped
2 garlic cloves, minced
3 ounces olive oil
½ teaspoon dried oregano
1 teaspoon black pepper

1 teaspoon cumin
4 ounces tomato paste
1 ounce dry sherry or cooking wine
4 ounces chicken broth
2 medium chickens, cleaned and halved
2 potatoes, peeled and halved
12 to 15 manzanillo olives (whole)

In a large skillet, cook the onion, bell pepper, and garlic in olive oil until tender. Add the oregano, black pepper, cumin, tomato paste, dry sherry, chicken broth, and 2½ cups of water. Add the chickens and let simmer for 45 minutes. Add the potatoes and olives and continue cooking for 20 minutes or until potatoes are soft.

SERVES 4

½ cebolla, picada
1 ají verde, picado
1 ají rojo, picado
2 ajos, picados finamente
80 gramos aceite de oliva
½ cucharita oregano
1 cucharita pimienta
1 cucharita comino

112 gramos pasta de tomate
28 gramos jerez seco o vino de cocinar
112 gramos caldo de pollo
2 pollos, tamaño mediano (limpiado y cortado)
2 papas, peladas y cortadas por la mitad
12 a 15 aceitunas manzanillo (enteras)

Cocinar la cebolla, ajies y ajo en el aceite de oliva hasta que se ablanden. Añadir oregano, pimienta, comino, pasta de tomate, vino de cocinar, caldo de pollo y 560 gramos de agua. Añadir el pollo y cocinar por 45 minutos. Añadir las papas y aceitunas y continuar cocinando por 20 minutos o hasta que las papas estén suaves.

SIRVE 4

"Cuban Food At Its Best"

TIRAMISU

½ pound mascarpone cheese
4 eggs, separated
½ cup sugar
1 cup cognac

25 ladyfingers
1 large cup black coffee
1 medium chocolate bar

Lightly butter the sides of an 8-inch mold. In a double boiler, or in a bowl over a pan of gently simmering water, mix the mascarpone with the egg yolks, sugar, and cognac until they form a thin ribbon. Cool over a larger pan filled with ice cubes and set aside.

In a separate bowl, beat the egg whites until stiff. Mix with the mascarpone cream. When you mix it, do not do it in a circular motion; rather, mix from the center toward the top, just until the egg whites are incorporated into the marscarpone mixture.

Soak the ladyfingers in the coffee and remove quickly so that the coffee doesn't overpower the flavor of the ladyfingers. In the mold, place a layer of the coffee-dipped ladyfingers along the bottom, cover with a layer of the mascarpone cream, another layer of ladyfingers, then a final layer of the cream.

Place in the refrigerator for several hours or overnight. To serve, shave the chocolate into curls and place over tiramisu.

SERVES 4

ONE THING TO KEEP IN MIND WITH THIS RECIPE—THE AMOUNT OF COGNAC YOU USE DEPENDS ON WHO YOU ARE MAKING THIS DESSERT FOR AND WHAT YOUR ULTIMATE INTENTIONS ARE.

ENJOY!

227 gramos queso mascarpone
4 huevos (las yemas separadas
  de las claras)
¼ taza azúcar

1 copita coñac
25 galletas "ladyfingers"
1 taza grande café negro
1 barra mediana de chocolate

Ligeramente engrase con mantequilla los lados de un molde de 20⅓ centímetros. En una olla doble (o puede usar un recipiente sobre una olla que tenga agua que esté ligeramente hirviendo) mezcle el mascarpone con las yemas, el azúcar y el coñac hasta que todo esté bien incorporado. Deje enfriar sobre otro recipiente que esté lleno de cubos de hielo y póngalo a un lado.

En un recipiente separado, bata las claras hasta que estén a punto de nieve. Mezcle con la crema de mascarpone. No lo mezcle con movimiento circular, sino que desde el centro hacia arriba, hasta que las claras se hayan incorporado a la mezcla de mascarpone.

Remoje las galletas en el café y quítelas rápidamente para que no quede muy fuerte el sabor a café. En el molde, ponga una capa de las galletas al fondo, cubra con una capa de crema de mascarpone, otra de galletas y finalmente una de crema.

Póngala en el refrigerador durante varias horas o durante la noche. Para servir, corte trozos rizados de chocolate y póngalos sobre el tiramisu.

SIRVE 4

Rafael Cisneros

RAFAEL CISNEROS WAS BORN ON JULY 16, 1963, IN EL SALVADOR. HE ARRIVED IN THE UNITED STATES IN AUGUST 1980, WHERE HE FINISHED HIGH SCHOOL, THEN ATTENDED THE UNIVERSITY OF THE DISTRICT OF COLUMBIA.

HE TRAINED UNDER THE INTERNATIONALLY KNOWN FRENCH CHEF YANNICK CAM FOR 11 YEARS AT LE PAVILION IN WASHINGTON, D.C. LATER, HE TRAINED IN ITALIAN CUISINE UNDER THE NATIONALLY RENOWNED CHEF ROBERTO DONNA. RAFAEL BECAME THE CHEF IN 1992 FOR PRIMI PIATTI IN TYSONS CORNER, VA., THEN AT IL CIGNO IN RESTON, VA. HE IS NOW WORKING FOR YANNICK CAM, CHEF/OWNER OF THE FAMOUS TRIO OF BEST RESTAURANTS IN WASHINGTON: PROVENCE, COCO LOCO, AND EL CATALAN. CISNEROS BECAME THE EXECUTIVE CHEF AT COCO LOCO, WHICH HOSTED THE OFFICIAL 1996 PRESIDENTIAL INAUGURAL BALL AND WON THE ZAGAT AWARD UNDER HIS DIRECTION FOR "BEST RESTAURANT OF 1996."

ESTUFADO DE AVESTRUZ (OSTRICH CASSEROLE)

FOR THE CASSEROLE:

2 pounds black beans

4 ounces oil

5 pounds ostrich, cut into cubes

5 pounds Mexican-style chorizo

Anchovy paste (to taste)

Cook the beans in oil in a large pot until tender. Leave them in their broth and set aside. Sauté the ostrich and the chorizo separately. Add the anchovy paste after the meats have a bit of color.

FOR THE SAUCE:

4 ounces oil

3 onions, chopped

12 cloves garlic, chopped

4 whole cloves

5 jalapeños, seeded and chopped

6 ancho chiles, seeded

Pinch ground cinnamon

Pinch ground cumin

6 arboles chiles

6 cups chicken broth

2 plantains, fried

In a frying pan over medium heat, sauté all the ingredients except the chicken broth and plantains until onions are translucent, about 4 minutes. Then add chicken broth, pour into a blender, and liquefy.

In a deep baking pan, mix the ostrich and chorizo with the sauce, then add the black beans in their broth, allowing them to thicken. Bake for 40 minutes in a 450-degree oven. Adorn with the fried plantains.

ESTUFADO DE AVESTRUZ

PARA LA CASEROLA:

1 kilogramo frijoles negros

112 gramos aceite

2¹/₃ kilogramos avestruz, picada en cubos

2¹/₃ kilogramos chorizo Mexicano

Pasta de anchoa (al gusto)

Cocinar los frijoles en una cazuela hasta que se ablanden. Dejar en sus jugos y poner a un lado. Saltear el avestruz y el chorizo separado. Añadir la pasta de anchoa después de que la carne tenga un poco de color.

PARA LA SALSA:

112 gramos aceite

3 cebollas, picadas

12 dientes de ajo, picados

4 clavo de olor

5 jalapeños (sin semilla y picados)

6 chiles anchos (sin semilla)

Pizca canela en polvo

Pizca comino en polvo

6 chiles de árbol

6 tazas caldo de pollo

2 plátanos fritos

Saltear todos los ingredientes, con la excepción del caldo de pollo y los plátanos, en un sartén sobre fuego medio hasta que las cebollas estén transparentes, casi 4 minutos. Poner en una batidora y licuar.

En un recipiente hondo, mezclar el avestruz y chorizo con la salsa, añadir los frijoles negros en su jugo y deje que espese. Cocinar por 45 minutos en un horno a 450 grados. Decorar con los plátanos fritos.

CHILES POBLANOS RELLENOS CON POLLO Y FRUTAS ABRILLANTADAS (CHILIES POBLANOS STUFFED WITH CHICKEN AND FRUIT)

FOR THE STUFFING:

10 poblano chilies, grilled and peeled
4 pounds chicken
3 ounces vegetable oil, about ¼ cup
    (divided into 2 parts)
1 tablespoon garlic, crushed
3 onions, julienned

4 ounces any dried fruit, chopped
4 ounces any golden raisins (dried)
10 leaves epazote, cut in quarters
1 pound Chihuahua cheese, shredded
4 large red tomatoes, seeded and
    finely chopped

Make a slit about 1 to 1½ inches long lengthwise in each chili. Grill the chilies until they puff up. Carefully peel the chilies under cold running water and pull out the membranes and seeds, making sure the chilies remain intact.

In a pot of water over medium/high heat, cook the chicken for 30 to 45 minutes. Let cool and shred chicken. Set aside.

In a saucepan, heat the oil, add the garlic, and cook for 5 seconds. Add the onions, fruit, raisins, and epazote and cook for 5 minutes. Remove from heat and let cool. Once cool, mix with the cheese and chicken and stuff the chilies carefully. Place in a baking pan and bake at 350 degrees for 5 to 7 minutes.

FOR THE SAUCE:

2 onions
1 pound walnuts, chopped
½ cup chicken broth
3 cups creme fraiche
Salt to taste

In a saucepan over medium heat, heat the remaining oil from the above recipe. Add the onions, and cook for 4 minutes. Then add the walnuts, chicken broth, creme fraiche, and salt. Heat through, then liquefy in blender.

FOR THE PRESENTATION:

2 pomegranates
1 plantain

Seed the pomegranates and set aside. Place a stuffed chili on each plate, spoon sauce over plate, and scatter the pomegranate seeds on top. Slice the plantain to use as a garnish around the plate.

CHILES POBLANOS RELLENOS CON POLLO
Y FRUTAS ABRILLANTADAS

Rafael Cisneros

PARA EL RELLENO:

10 chiles poblanos (asado y pelado)
2 kilogramos pollo
80 gramos aceite de vegetal
1 cucharada ajo molido
3 cebollas, picada
112 gramos fruta secada, picada

112 gramos pasas doradas, secadas
10 hojas epazote, cortada en cuartos
454 gramos queso Chihuahua, cortada
4 tomates rojos grandes, sin semilla
　　y picada fina

Hacer una cortada en cada chile de 2½ a 3¾ centímetros a lo largo. Asar los chiles hasta que cominezan a abrir. Con cuidado, pelar los chiles bajo agua fria, y sacar las semillas, asegurando que se queden intactos.

En un sartén hondo sobre fuego medio/alto cocinar el pollo por 30 a 45 minutos. Dejar enfriar y deshebrar el pollo y poner a un lado.

En un sartén, calentar el aceite, añadir el ajo y cocinar por 5 segundos. Añadir la cebolla, fruta, pasas y epazote y cocinar por 5 minutos. Remover del fuego y dejar enfriar. Cuando este frío, mezclar con el queso y rellenar los chiles con cuidado. Poner en un recipiente y hornear por 5 a 7 minutos a 350 grados F.

PARA LA SALSA:

2 cebollas
454 gramos nueces, picadas
½ taza caldo de pollo
3 tazas creme fraiche
Sal (al gusto)

En un sartén sobre fuego medio, calentar el aceite y añadir la cebolla y cocinar por 4 minutos. Añadir las nueces, sal, caldo de pollo y creme fraiche. Cocinar y poner en una licuadora.

PARA LA PRESENTACION:

2 granadas
1 plátano

Sacar las semillas de las granadas y poner a un lado. Poner un chile relleno en cada plato para servir, poner un poco de la salsa sobre el plato y poner las semillas de las granadas encima. Poner los plátanos como adorno alrededor del plato.

Luis Contreras

BORN AND RAISED IN CARACAS, VENEZUELA, LUIS CONTRERAS HAS MADE HIS HOME IN MIAMI FOR THE PAST 25 YEARS. HE GRADUATED FROM THE SCHOOL OF CUISINE CHEFS AT THE CULINARY INSTITUTE OF AMERICA IN NEW YORK. HE HAS WORKED IN SEVERAL PRESTIGIOUS RESTAURANTS IN SOUTH FLORIDA, INCLUDING GIACOSA IN CORAL GABLES AND STEFANO'S RESTAURANT IN KEY BISCAYNE AS WELL AS BELLINI'S RESTAURANT ON CAPTIVA ISLAND. LUIS WAS ALSO EXECUTIVE CHEF OF YUCA RESTAURANT IN CORAL GABLES.

THE INNOVATIVE CUBAN CUISINE THAT IS YUCA'S TRADEMARK WILL BE LIFTED TO NEW HEIGHTS AS LUIS BRINGS WITH HIM A UNIQUE STYLE AND CREATIVE ENERGY THAT WILL DELIGHT PATRONS OF THE ALREADY PRESTIGIOUS AND INTERNATIONALLY ACCLAIMED YUCA RESTAURANT ON LINCOLN ROAD IN MIAMI BEACH.

CEVICHE COCOMAR

½ pound small scallops
½ pound firm-fleshed fish, diced
   (e.g. grouper, dolphin, sea bass)
½ pound medium shrimp, peeled
½ pound calamari
Cilantro for garnish

FOR THE MARINADE:
1 whole tomato, roasted
1 whole red pepper, roasted and seeded
1 whole jalapeño, roasted and seeded
2 cups fresh squeezed lime juice, strained
1 can coconut milk

Combine all the marinade ingredients and puree in a blender.

In a pot of boiling water, add the scallops and cook for 1 minute; add the fish and cook for another minute; add the shrimp and cook for one more minute; add the calamari and cook for 30 seconds. Strain all the seafood, then plunge into an ice bath and put the cold seafood into the marinade. Serve in halved coconut shells and garnish with fresh chopped cilantro.

SERVES 4

---

250 gramos veneras pequeñas
250 gramos pescado firme picado
   (eje. delfín, lenguado, pescado rojo)
250 gramos camarones, pelado
250 gramos calamar
Cilantro (a decorear)

PARA MARINAR:
1 tomate entero, rostizado
1 pimiento entero, rostizado y sin semillas
1 jalapeño entero, rostizado y sin semillas
2 tazas jugo de lima fresco, colado
1 lata leche de coco

Combine todos los ingredientes para marinar y hágalos puré en la licuadora.

En una cazuela de agua hirviendo, agregar las veneras, cocinar por un minuto, agregue el pescado y cocine por otro minuto, agregue el camarones y cocine por otro minuto más, agregue el calamar y cocine por 30 segundos. Cuele todos los mariscos y después póngalos en un baño de hielo y después ponga los mariscos frios en la el jugo para marinar, sirva en cascos de coco y adorne con cilantro fresco.

SIRVE 4

SOPA DE FRIJOLES NEGROS (BLACK BEAN SOUP)

3 pounds black beans, sorted and
   cleaned, and water to cover 3 inches
   over beans
3 bay leaves
3 cups Sofrito (recipe below)
1 cup olive oil

½ cup chopped garlic
1 tablespoon dried oregano
1 tablespoon ground cumin
2 tablespoons salt
½ cup sugar

Cook the beans with the bay leaves until tender (about 1 hour, less if you soak the beans overnight). Add water if needed. Add Sofrito. Cook garlic slowly in olive oil, then add to beans. Add dry seasonings. Simmer soup for 45 minutes. In a serving bowl, garnish the soup with sour cream, chopped onions, scallions, or your own favorites.

FOR THE SOFRITO:
4 red bell peppers, cleaned
2 onions, quartered

Olive oil
1 cup garlic cloves, whole

Cook the peppers and onions in olive oil over low heat until tender (about 45 minutes). Add garlic cloves and cook an additional 15 minutes. Season with salt and black pepper to taste and puree in a blender.

1½ kilogramos frijoles negros, limpios y con
   7½ a 8 centímetros de agua sobre
   los frijoles
3 hojas de laurel
3 tazas Sofrito (receta abajo)
1 taza aceite de oliva

½ taza de ajo picado (cocidos juntos)
1 cucharada orégano seco
1 cucharada comino en polvo
2 cucharada sal
½ taza azúcar

Cocinar los frijoles con hojas de laurel hasta que se ablanden (como una hora, menos si los remoja durante la noche). Agregue agua si es necesario. Agregue Sofrito. Cocine ajo despacio en el aceite de oliva y después agregue los frijoles. Agregue todos los condimentos. Cocine la sopa durante 45 minutos más. En un plato hondo decore la sopa con crema agria, cebollas picadas, sebollines, o cualquiera de sus favoritos.

POR EL SOFRITO:
4 pimientos rojos, lavados
1 cebolla, cortada en cuadros

Aceite de oliva
1 taza dientes de ajo, enteros

Cocinar los pimientos y las cebollas en aceite de oliva hasta que estén blandos (como 45 minutos). Agregue gajos de ajos y cocine por 15 minutos más. Condimente con sal y pimienta al gusto y bata en la batidora.

SALAD OF PURPLE POTATOES AND POACHED SHRIMP IN A COCO-LIME VINAIGRETTE

FOR THE POACHED SHRIMP:
2 cups white wine
1 bay leaf
1 teaspoon peppercorns
4 cloves garlic
1 tablespoon crab boil
1½ pounds medium-sized shrimp
    (21 to 25, peeled and cleaned)

Combine first five ingredients and bring to a boil. Simmer for 2 minutes. Add the shrimp, stir and bring to a simmer, cook until opaque (just done), and remove from heat. Add a bowl of ice to the hot liquid and stir well until cool. Let sit in poaching liquid for at least one hour.

FOR THE COCO-LIME VINAIGRETTE:
1 can coconut milk
Pinch salt
Pinch sugar
Juice from 4 large limes
2 stalks lemon grass
½ cup light olive oil

In a blender, combine all ingredients except oil and blend well. Drizzle in the oil until blended well.

FOR THE PRESENTATION:
4 boiled purple potatoes (substitute white potatoes if not available), cooled and diced
1 scallion, sliced on bias
2 dry coconut halves

Combine potatoes, shrimp, coco-lime dressing, and scallions in a bowl and toss well. Present in coconut shells and garnish with scallions.

ENSALADA CON PAPAS MORADAS Y CAMARONES COCIDOS EN UNA VINAGRETA DE COCO-LIMA

PARA LOS CAMARONES COCIDOS:
2 tazas vino blanco
1 hoja de laurel
1 cucharita granos de pimienta
4 dientes de ajo
1 cucharada consomé de cangrejo
680 gramos camarones medianos (pelados y lavados de 21-25)

Combine y hierva los primeros 5 ingredientes. Hervir a fuego lento por 2 minutos. Agregue el camarón, mezcle y deje hervir a fuego lento hasta que el cocido se vea opaco (exacto cocido), retire del fuego. Agregue el equivalente de un plato hondo de hielo al jugo y mezclar hasta que esté frío. Déjelo reposar en el jugo por lo menos una hora.

PARA LA VINAGRETA COCO-LIMA:
1 lata leche de coco
Pizca sal
Pizca azúcar
Jugo de 4 limas
2 ramillas de limón
½ taza aceite de oliva de grasa reducida

En una batidora, combine todos los ingredientes, excepto el aceite y bata bien todos los ingredientes. Esparcir sobre le aceite hasta que se mezcle bien.

PARA PRESENTACIÓN:
4 papas moradas (sustituya papas blancas si no las hay disponibles),
    enfríe y corte en cuadritos
1 cebollita verde cortada en diagonal
2 mitades de coco seco

Combine las papas con los camarones, aderezo de coco-lima y las cebollitas en un tazón y revolver. Preséntelo en las mitades de coco y decore con las cebollitas.

Michael Cordua

CORN-SMOKED CRAB FINGERS AND SCALLOPS WITH GRILLED MUSHROOMS

6 to 8 dried corn husks
1 (8½ x 11-inch) covered, stainless-steel stovetop smoker or a 1 x 16 x 3-inch disposable aluminum roasting pan and an 8 x 12-inch cooling rack

8 large sea scallops
2 pounds fresh crab fingers or 1 pound shelled Dungeness whole crab legs
8 large mushroom caps
Olive oil

Place corn husks in the bottom of the smoker. Fill liquids pan with desired liquid and set inside smoker. Arrange the scallops and crab fingers evenly on grill. Add cover to seal in smoke. If using roasting pan, place husks in bottom of pan and place a 9 x 15-inch rectangle of aluminum foil over husks, leaving a 1-inch border to allow smoke to escape. Place the cooling rack on top of the foil. Cover with foil and perforate to facilitate smoking. Arrange the scallops and crab fingers evenly over the perforated foil. Cover with the foil and seal to trap the smoke.

Place smoker or roasting pan on top of the stove over medium heat. The husks start to burn almost immediately and the smoke flavors and cooks the ingredients in 3 to 5 minutes. Remove from heat and reserve. Baste the mushrooms with olive oil. Broil on grill for 2 minutes. Season with salt and pepper. Reserve.

FOR THE HUANCAINA SAUCE:

½ tablespoon olive oil
½ large red bell pepper, coarsely chopped
1 red jalapeño, coarsely chopped
¼ onion, coarsely chopped

2 tablespoons dry sherry
5 ounces evaporated milk
¾ cup grated Cotija or farmer's cheese
1 cup whipping cream

In a sauté pan over medium heat, heat olive oil and sauté the red bell pepper, jalapeño, and onion until softened, about 3 to 5 minutes. Add the sherry and continue to cook 1 minute more. Transfer sautéed vegetables to a blender. Add the evaporated milk and cheese. Puree. Return to sauté pan and add the whipping cream. Cook until thickened, 3 to 5 minutes, and strain. Reserve.

TO SERVE:

Coat center of dinner plate with Huancaina Sauce. Place one smoked scallop inside each mushroom cap and put in center of plate. Arrange smoked crab fingers in a circle around each stuffed mushroom cap. Serve immediately.

MAÍZ AHUMADO DEDOS DE CANGREJO Y VENERAS CON HONGOS ASADOS A LA PARRILLA

6-8 hojas de maíz secas

1 (8½ x 11 pulgadas, 21½ x 28 centímetros) caja de acero cubierta con parrilla para ahumar o una cacerola de aluminio de 11 x 16 x 3 pulgadas (28 x 40³/5 x 7³/5 centímetros) disponible y una parrilla de 8 x 12 pulgadas (20¹/3 x 30½ centímetros)

8 veneras

1 kilogramo dedos de cangrejo frescos o 454 gramos de piernas de cangrejo sin concha

8 capas de champiñones

Aceite de oliva

Coloque las hojas de maíz en el fondo del ahumador. Llene la cacerola con jugos deseados y ponga la cacerola dentro del ahumador. Arregle las veneras y los dedos de cangrejo iguales en la parrilla. Agregue la tapadera para tapar el humo. Si usa la cacerola de aluminio; coloque las hojas en el fondo de la cacerola, ponga un rectangulo de aluminio de aproximadamente 9 x 15 pulgadas (23 x 38 centímetros) encima de las hojas, deje una pulgada (2½ centímetros) para que el humo pueda escapar. Coloque la parrilla arriba del aluminio. Cubra la parrilla con aluminio perforado para facilitar el humo. Arregle veneras y dedos de cangrejo iguales con aluminio perforado. Cúbralos y ciérrelos con aluminio para encerrar el humo.

Coloque el ahumador o la cacerola de aluminio encima de la estufa sobre fuego medio. Las hojas comienzan a quemar casi inmediatamente y los sabores del humo cocinan los ingredientes entre 3 a 5 minutos. Remueva del fuego y reserve. Aderece los champiñones con aceite de oliva. Sazone con sal y pimienta. Guarde.

PARA LA SALSA DE HUANCAINA:

½ cucharada de aceite de olivo

½ aji grande rojo, cortado grueso

1 chile jalapeño rojo, cortado grueso

¼ cebolla, cortado grueso

2 cucharadas de vino de jerez

140 gramos leche evaporada

¾ taza queso rallado, Cotija o queso granjero

1 taza nata líquida (crema para batir)

En una cacerola encima del fuego, caliente el aceite de olivo y saltée el chile rojo, jalapeño y cebolla hasta que estén blandos aproximadamente 3 a 5 minutos. Agregue el jerez y continúe cociéndolo por un minuto más. Ponga los vegetales salteados en la licuadora. Agregue leche evaporada y queso rallado. Puré. Regrese a la cacerola y agregue la crema. Cocine hasta que esté espeso 3 a 5 minutos y pase por un colador. Guarde.

SERVIR:

Cubra el centro de cada plato con la salsa de Hunancaina. Coloque una venera ahumada dentro de cada capa de champiñón y coloque en el centro del plato. Arregle los dedos de cangrejo ahumados en un círculo alrededor de cada capa de champiñón relleno. Sirva inmediatamente.

Michael Cordua

OF LATIN AMERICAN CUISINE AND UTILIZE THE ABUNDANCE OF OUR OWN HIGH-QUALITY AMERICAN INGREDIENTS. AT THE 1994 FOOD & WINE CLASSIC, CORDUA BECAME ONLY THE SECOND HOUSTON CHEF (AFTER ROBERT McGRATH '88) TO BE NAMED ONE OF AMERICA'S "TEN BEST NEW CHEFS" BY FOOD & WINE.

MICHAEL WAS ALSO THE RECIPIENT OF THE 1994 ROBERT MONDAVI AWARD FOR CULINARY EXCELLENCE. THIS MARKED THE FIRST YEAR FOR THE AWARD, WHICH WENT TO 13 "RISING STAR" CHEFS THROUGHOUT THE UNITED STATES, AS ELECTED BY SOME OF THE TOP CULINARY FIGURES IN THE NATION.

ANOTHER OF MICHAEL'S BUSINESS VENTURES IS HIS NEW LINE OF GOURMET SAUCES AND PLANTAIN CHIPS INTENDED FOR THE RETAIL MARKET. THE "FLAVORS OF THE RAINFOREST" BRAND OF PRODUCTS WAS INTRODUCED IN TIME FOR THE 1994 CHRISTMAS MARKET. A BLACK-AND-WHITE COWHIDE BRIEFCASE-SHAPED BOX IS FILLED WITH SEVEN-OUNCE JARS OF SALSA MIREYA, A TANGY-SWEET PEPPER SAUCE; CHIMICHURRI SAUCE, A GARLICKY BASTING SAUCE; AND A FAT-FREE AMAZON DRESSING, A CREAMY CILANTRO-FLAVORED SALAD DRESSING, AND A BAG OF CRISPY FRIED PLANTAIN CHIPS.

MICHAEL AND HIS WIFE, LUCIA, ALSO A GRADUATE OF TEXAS A&M UNIVERSITY, ARE THE PARENTS OF FOUR CHILDREN. A

Michael Cordua

DEVOTED FAMILY MAN, MICHAEL HAS SELECTED CASA DE ESPERANZA, A NON-PROFIT CRISIS CENTER FOR HIV-POSITIVE INFANTS AND CHILDREN UNDER SIX WHO ARE AT RISK, AS THE BENEFICIARY OF A NUMBER OF CHARITABLE GALAS HELD AT HIS RESTAURANTS. TO DATE, THESE GALAS HAVE RAISED MORE THAN $500,000 FOR THIS WORTHY CAUSE.

TIRITAS (POTATO-CRUSTED FILLETS OF CALAMARI)

1¼ pounds calamari, cleaned
Salt and black pepper
1½ cups flour
1½ cups egg wash (egg mixed
   with equal parts water)

10 ounces potato chips, crushed into small
   pieces
Peanut oil for frying

Cut calamari into strips; season with salt and pepper. Place flour and egg wash in separate bowls. Toss calamari in flour, then egg wash, removing any excess. Toss the strips in the crushed potato chips. Heat peanut oil in frying pan and deep fry the coated strips. Serve with jalapeño mayonnaise and spicy ketchup.

FOR THE JALAPEÑO MAYONNAISE:

2 cups mayonnaise
Juice of 1 lime
Salt and black pepper
2 tablespoons onion, finely diced

2 tablespoons red bell pepper, finely diced
1 jalapeño pepper, finely diced
2 tablespoons green onion, finely diced
2 tablespoons cilantro, finely diced

Mix first 3 ingredients together. Blend in remaining ingredients and chill.

FOR THE SPICY KETCHUP:

2 cups ketchup
¼ teaspoon or more cayenne pepper

Juice of 1½ limes

Mix ingredients together and chill.

---

570 gramos calamar limpio
Sal y pimienta
1½ tazas harina
1½ tazas lavado de huevo (huevos
   mezclados con partes iguales de agua)

280 gramos papitas fritas, trituradas
   en pequeñas piezas
Aceite de cacahuate para freír

Cortar calamar en tiritas y sazonar con sal y pimienta. Poner la harina con el huevo en recipientes separados. Vierta el calamar en la harina, después al huevo, removiendo cualquier exceso. Caliente el aceite de cacahuate en una sartén. Agregue las tiras sobre las papitas fritas y fría en aceite de cacahuate. Sirva con mayonesa de jalapeño y con salsa de tomate picante.

PARA LA MAYONESA DE JALAPEÑO:

2 tazas mayonesa
Jugo de 1 lima
Sal y pimienta
2 cucharadas cebolla, finamente picada

2 cucharadas pimiento rojo, finamente picado
1 chile Jalapeño, finamente picado
2 cucharadas cebollitas, finamente picadas
2 cucharadas cilantro, finamente picado

Mezcle los primeros 3 ingredientes. Batir los ingredientes restantes y enfríe.

PARA EL "KETCHUP" (SALSA DE TOMATE) PICANTE:

2 tazas ketchup
¼ cucharita o más pimienta cheyene

Jugo de 1½ limas

Mezcle todo y enfríe.

RELLENOS DE PORRAS

Michael Cordua

8 ounces raisins
4 cups milk
1 loaf white bread
2 pounds pork loin, cubed
½ pound salt pork, cubed
1 onion, chopped
4 cloves garlic
1 cup pimiento-stuffed green olives
3 tablespoons capers
1 tablespoon Worcestershire sauce

2 tablespoons ketchup
1 teaspoon nutmeg
4 teaspoons ginger
2 tablespoons mustard
1 pound potatoes, cubed and cooked
2 eggs, beaten
4 tablespoons vinegar
2 tablespoons sugar
1 cup butter
Salt and black pepper

Soak raisins in a bowl in 1 cup of milk overnight. Tear the bread into bite-sized pieces; place in a large bowl with 3 cups milk. Soak both overnight in refrigerator. In a large pot of water, boil pork loin, salt pork, onion, garlic, and salt to taste for 25 to 30 minutes. When the meat is whitish and not pink, drain, reserving liquid.

Coarsely chop the boiled ingredients. Be sure to retain the integrity of the meat; do not turn it to paste. In a very large bowl, mix the remaining ingredients except the butter with the chopped and boiled meat. Strain the reserved liquid and add to dressing mixture. Melt butter in a large nonstick skillet. Cook the dressing in the melted butter, stirring frequently until golden brown, about 4 hours. Add more butter as needed. Taste and adjust seasonings.

---

224 gramos pasas
4 tazas leche
1 barra pan blanco
1 kilogramo lomo de puerco, en cubos
250 gramos puerco salado, en cubos
1 cebolla picada
4 gajos ajo
1 taza aceitunas verdes rellenas de pimiento
3 cucharadas alcaparras
1 cucharada salsa Worcestershire

2 cucharadas ketchup
1 cucharita nuez moscada
4 cucharitas jengibre
2 cucharadas mostaza
450 gramos papas cocidas en cubos
2 huevos, batidos
4 cucharadas vinagre
2 cucharadas azúcar
1 taza mantequilla
Sal y pimienta

En un pequeño recipiente, remojar las pasas en una taza de leche durante la noche. Corte el pan en trozos pequeños, en un recipiente grande con 3 tazas de leche. Deje reposar ambos durante la noche en el refrigerados. En una olla grande de agua, hierva el lomo y el puerco salado, cebolla, ajo y sal por 25 a 30 minutos. Cuando la carne se vea blanquisca y no rosa, quitar el caldo, y guardar el caldito.

Machaque en trozos los ingredientes que ha hervido. Asegúrese de la integridad de la carne; no la haga pastosa. En una recipiente grande, mezclar todos los ingredientes excepto la mantequilla con las carnes machacadas. Cuele el caldillo y agregue a la mezcla de aderezo. Derrita la mantequilla en un sartén de fondo resistente, y de preferencia de teflón. Cocine en la mantequilla derretida, mezclando constantemente, hasta que esté dorado, como unas cuatro horas. Agregue mas mantequilla como la vaya necesitanto. Pruebelo y ajuste los condimentos.

Celia Cruz

I LOVE GINGER. I USE IT IN EVERY-THING—GINGER AND RICE, GINGER AND PLATANOS. I EVEN USE GINGER IN MY WATER. MY OTHER PASSION IS SEAFOOD, BECAUSE IT'S DELICIOUS AND EASY TO PREPARE. TOGETHER, THIS GINGER SHRIMP RECIPE BRINGS ME TO HEAVEN, AND I HOPE TO TAKE YOU ON THAT SAME JOURNEY.

CAMARONES JENGIBRE (GINGER SHRIMP)

1 tablespoon extra virgin olive oil
12 large shrimp
Salt and black pepper
1 medium onion, chopped
¼ cup fresh lime juice
2 tablespoons scallions, minced

2 tablespoons fresh cilantro
1 tablespoon fresh ginger, minced
2 tablespoons rough brown sugar
   (divided in half)
1 large pineapple, sliced

Heat olive oil in skillet. Season shrimp to taste with salt and pepper. Add onion and continue cooking for 2 minutes more. Stir in 2 tablespoons lime juice, the scallions, and the cilantro. Let cool.

In a bowl, combine the remaining lime juice with the ginger, half the brown sugar, salt, and pepper. Add the pineapple slices to the mixture and marinate at room temperature for an hour. Preheat broiler. Broil the pineapple slices for about 2 minutes on each side or until lightly browned. Cut each piece into four and arrange on individual plates with three of the shrimp. Put a spoonful of ginger marinade over all and sprinkle with the remaining brown sugar.

SERVES 4

---

1 cucharada aceite de oliva
12 camarones grandes
Sal y pimienta
1 cebolla mediana, cortada
¼ taza jugo de limón verde
2 cucharadas cebollitas verdes, cortadas
   finamente

2 cucharadas cilantro fresco
1 cucharada jengibre, cortado
2 cucharadas azúcar moreno
1 piña, cortada a lo largo

Calienta el aceite en el sartén. Sazonar los camarones al gusto con sal y pimienta. Añadir la cebolla y cocinar por 2 minutos. Mezclar 2 cucharas de jugo de limón verde, cebollitas y cilantro. Retira del fuego y déjalo enfriar.

En una cazuela, combina el resto del jugo de limón verde con el jengibre, azúcar, sal, y pimienta. Ponga la mezcla en la piña y deja reposar una hora. Ponga a asar la piña por dos minutos en cada lado. Corta cada pedazo en cuatro y divide en platos individuales con tres camarones por plato. Ponga encima la mezcla de jengibre y un poco de azúcar moreno.

SIRVE 4

SHRIMP SALAD PIONONO WITH CALABAZA SEED VINAIGRETTE

FOR THE SHRIMP SALAD:

4 tablespoons Cajun seasoning
18 medium-sized (16-20) deveined raw shrimp
1½ heads frisee lettuce
3 bunches assorted lettuce
1 cup Calabaza Seed Vinaigrette
   (recipe follows)

12 Pionono Shells
Plantain chips for garnish
Cilantro Oil, Annatto Oil,
   Balsamic Glaze to decorate
   (recipes follow)

In a small mixing bowl, mix the shrimp with the Cajun seasoning, then grill. Set aside to cool and then coarsely chop. Fill up a mixing bowl with ice water and wash the lettuce. Let it sit in ice water for 2 minutes. Dry lettuce and set aside.

FOR THE PIONONO SHELL:

2 plátanos amarillos (ripe plantains)
¼ medium-sized potato

Peel the ripe plantains and slice them ⅛-inch thick lengthwise. Peel the potato and cut into 1-inch-long and ⅛-inch-thick matchsticks. Form a plantain slice into a circle and "staple" with the potato sticks from one side to another. Proceed to do the same with the rest of the plantain slices. Spread the plantains on a preheated fryer at 350 degrees and fry for 2 to 3 minutes. Drain on paper towels and set aside.

FOR THE CALABAZA SEED VINAIGRETTE:

2 tablespoons calabaza or pumpkin seeds
2 tablespoons shallots, chopped
1 tablespoon garlic, chopped
1 tablespoon red onion, chopped

2 tablespoons cilantro, chopped
1 tablespoon chives, chopped
¼ cup white vinegar
¾ cup olive oil

Toast calabaza or pumpkin seeds in preheated 350-degree oven for 5 minutes. In a mixing bowl, add all the ingredients except the vinegar and oil. Add vinegar slowly and whisk in the oil until well mixed. Yields 8 ounces.

FOR THE CILANTRO OIL:

1 bunch cilantro
½ cup vegetable oil

Pinch salt
Pinch black pepper

Finely chop cilantro, then blend or whisk together with oil. Add salt and pepper.

FOR THE ANNATTO OIL:

½ cup grape seed oil
¼ cup annatto seeds

In a saucepan, heat the oil and seeds together over low heat until the oil just begins to bubble—this takes 8 to 10 minutes. Remove and set aside for 1 hour.

Jeremie Cruz

WHEN THE EXECUTIVE CHEF AT EL CONQUISTADOR RESORT AND COUNTRY CLUB WAS LOOKING FOR A RESTAURANT CHEF FOR THE *NUEVO LATINO* CONCEPT, CASSAVE RESTAURANT, HE SET HIS EYES ON JEREMIE CRUZ. HE HAS BEEN A GREAT ASSET AT THIS RESORT.

JEREMIE WAS BORN AND RAISED ON THE BEAUTIFUL ISLAND OF PUERTO RICO. SINCE CHILDHOOD HE WAS INTERESTED IN LEARNING HOW TO COOK THE TYPICAL FOOD OF HIS NATION. AS YEARS WENT BY, THIS PASSION KEPT GROWING INSIDE HIM, SO EARLY ON, HE LEARNED HOW TO PLAY WITH INGREDIENTS AND CREATE DIFFERENT DISHES.

AT THE AGE OF 17, HE STARTED WORKING AT A BAKE SHOP IN CEIBA, PUERTO RICO, AND AT 18, HE GOT A JOB AS A PREP COOK AT ISABELA'S RESTAURANT, A MEDITERRANEAN RESTAURANT AT EL CONQUISTADOR. TWO MONTHS LATER, HE WAS PROMOTED TO COMMIS I. THE WORKING HOURS WERE LONG BUT EVENTUALLY PAID OFF WHEN, JUST EIGHT MONTHS LATER, HE BECAME A CULINARY

MANAGEMENT TRAINEE (CMT) AND WAS GRANTED A SCHOLARSHIP TO STUDY ADVANCED COURSES OF CULINARY ARTS AT THE CULINARY INSTITUTE OF AMERICA. IN 1995 AND 1996, WHILE JEREMIE WAS WORKING AT ISABELA'S, THE RESTAURANT RECEIVED A TRIPLE A, 4 DIAMOND AWARD.

JEREMIE WAS SELECTED AS PART OF THE PUERTO RICAN NATIONAL CULINARY TEAM TO COMPETE AT THE CARIBBEAN CULINARY COMPETITION IN SEPTEMBER 1997. IN THE MEANTIME, HE KEEPS HIMSELF BUSY PARTICIPATING IN COMPETITIONS AND MAKING SURE ALL GUESTS WHO VISIT CASSAVE RESTAURANT ARE PAMPERED AND HAVE AN UNSURPASSED QUALITY EXPERIENCE, ONE THAT THEY WILL REMEMBER AND TELL THEIR FRIENDS ABOUT.

FOR THE BALSAMIC GLAZE:

7½ ounces balsamic vinegar   3 ounces sugar

Mix vinegar and sugar together in a saucepan and reduce on medium-low heat ¼ of the way. Set aside to cool off.

TO SERVE:

Mix lettuce and shrimp with vinaigrette in a mixing bowl, then fill up piononos with the salad. Place the three piononos in the center of plate in a triangle form. Garnish with chips on center and oils around the plate.

SERVES 4

ENSALADA DE CAMARÓN PIONONO CON SEMILLA DE CALABAZA VINAGRETA

PARA LA ENSALADA DE CAMARÓN:

4 cucharas sazonamiento Cajún

18 camarones medianos (16-20) crudo desvenado

1½ cabeza lechuga frisee

3 diferentes manojos de lechugas

1 taza Vinagreta de Semilla de Calabaza (receta sigue)

12 cada conchas de pionono

Trozos de plátano

Aceite de Cilantro, Aceite de Annatto, Glaseado Balsamico para decorar (recetas siguen)

En un pequeño cuenco, mezcle camarón crudo con sazonamiento Cajún. En una parrilla los camarones son asados. Póngalos a un lado para que se tibien y despúes córtelos. Llene un cuenco con agua helada, limpie las lechugas y déjelas que en el agua helada por dos minutos. Seque las lechugas y póngalas a un lado.

PARA LA CONCHA DE PIONONOS:

2 plátanos amarillos

¼ papa mediana

Pele los plátanos maduros y corte en ³⁄₁₀ centímetro largas. Pele la papa y corte en trozos de 2½ centímetros de largo y ³⁄₁₀ centímetro de ancho. Doble los plátanos en un círculo y grapa con los trozos, de papa de un lado al otro. Proceda a hacer lo mismo con el resto de las rodajas de plátanos. Póngalos en un sartén previamente calentado a 350 grados F, los plátanos se fríen por dos a tres minutos. Séquelos en toallas de papel y pongalos a un lado.

PARA LA VINAGRETA DE SEMILLA DE CALABAZA :

2 cucharas semilla de calabaza

2 cucharas de chalote cortado

1 cuchara de ajo cortado

1 cuchara cebolla roja cortado

2 cucharas cilantro cortado

1 cuchara cebollino cortado

¼ taza vinagre blanco

¾ taza aceite de oliva

Tueste las semillas de calabaza en un horno previamente calentado en 350 grados F por 5 minutos. En un cuenco, ponga todos los ingredientes excepto el vinagre y aceite. Agregue el vinagre bien despacio y revuelva en el aceite hasta que estén bien mezclados. Rinde 228 gramos.

PARA EL ACEITE DE CILANTRO:

1 manojo de cilantro
½ taza aceite vegetal

Una pizca de sal
Una pizca de pimienta

Corte muy finito el cilantro, entonces mezcle o bata junto con el aceite. Agregue sal y pimienta hasta que estén bien mezclados.

PARA EL ACEITE DE ANNATTO:

½ taza aceite de semilla de uva

½ taza semillas de annatto

En una olla caliente el aceite y semillas juntos sobre un fuego bajo, hasta que el aceite empiece a burbujar, ésto toma aproximadamente 8 a 10 minutos. Quite del fuego y ponga a un lado por una hora.

PARA EL GLASEADO BALSAMICO:

210 gramos de vinagre balsámico

84 gramos de azucar

Mezcla juntos en una olla reduzca a fuego medio en ¼ del proceso. Ponga aparte para que se pueda enfriar.

PARA SERVIR:

Mezcle lechugas y camarónes con la vinagreta, en un cuenco, llene los piononos con la ensalada. Ponga los tres piononos en el centro del plato en forma de triángulo. Decore con los totopos en medio y aceites alrededor del plato.

SIRVE 4

LAMB CHOPS WITH MOFONGO AND CILANTRO PESTO

FOR THE LAMB CHOPS:

8 double lamb chops
Salt and black pepper to taste
12 ounces mofongo (recipe follows)
4 ounces cilantro pesto (recipe follows)

2 ounces Chimichurri sauce
  (recipe follows)
Plantain chips (for garnish)

FOR THE MOFONGO:

3 large green plantains
3 cups water, salted with ½ tablespoon salt
½ tablespoon bacon, diced
3 cloves garlic, minced

½ cup extra virgin olive oil
¼ teaspoon Cassave seasoning
Salt and black pepper to taste
¼ cup corn oil

Peel the plantains and cut into ½-inch slices. Place them into the salted water. Sauté the bacon; drain and discard the fat. Chop coarsely and set aside. Combine the garlic, olive oil, and Cassave seasoning. Heat the corn oil and fry the plantain slices until golden brown. Drain on paper towels. Place a few teaspoons of garlic oil in a bowl. Add ⅙ of the bacon and 5 or 6 slices of plantain. Mash and press firmly into a mortar and pestle. Keep warm.

FOR THE CILANTRO PESTO:

2 cups cilantro
¾ cup olive oil
½ cup grated Parmesan cheese
1 teaspoon Cassave seasoning

2 tablespoons lemon juice
⅓ cup walnuts, chopped
4 cloves garlic
Pinch salt and black pepper

Combine all ingredients in food processor and blend until smooth but chunky.

FOR THE CHIMICHURRI SAUCE:

2 cloves garlic
1 bay leaf
1 jalapeño pepper, coarsely chopped, with seeds
½ tablespoon salt
⅛ cup fresh parsley, minced

⅛ cup flat-leaf parsley, minced
⅛ cup fresh cilantro, minced
2 tablespoon Jamaican jerk seasoning
¼ cup extra virgin olive oil
⅛ cup distilled white vinegar

Mix the ingredients for chimichurri in a mortar and pestle until a smooth paste is formed (or you can puree with a small amount of vinegar in a blender). Transfer to a mixing bowl and add jerk seasoning. Whisk in the olive oil and vinegar until well mixed and set aside. Divide it in half—one for the sauce and the other to marinate the lamb chops.

FOR THE LATIN ROOT VEGETABLES:

2 cups purple potatoes, diced
2 cups calabaza, diced
2 cups chayote, diced
2 cups celery, diced

2 cups malanga, diced
1 teaspoon olive oil
1 teaspoon garlic, minced
Salt and black pepper to taste

Blanch all the vegetables for a minute in boiling water, then sauté in olive oil with garlic and season to taste. Set aside.

TO SERVE:

In an ovenproof pan or on a flat top, quickly sear the lamb chops on all sides. Place in a preheated 425-degree oven and roast until meat reaches an internal temperature of 120 degrees for medium rare.

Invert hot mofongo into center of a warm plate. Place the lamb chops leaning against the mofongo. Decorate with sautéed root vegetables around the plate, the pesto on the chops, and sauces drizzled on the plate. Finish with a plantain chip positioned behind.

SERVES 4

CHULETA DE CORDERO CON MOFONGO Y CILANTRO PESTO

Jeremie Cruz

PARA LA CHULETA DE CORDERO:

8 chuletas de cordero doble
Sal y pimienta al gusto
330 gramos mofongo (receta sigue)
112 gramos pesto de cilantro (receta sigue)

56 gramos de salsa Chimichurri (receta sigue)
Trozos de plátano (para decorar)

PARA EL MOFONGO:

3 plátanos grandes verdes
3 tazas agua, salada con ½ cuchara sal
½ cuchara tocino picado
3 dientes de ajo, picados

½ taza aceite de oliva virgen
¼ cucharilla sazonamiento del Cassave
Sal y pimienta al gusto
¼ taza aceite de maíz

Pele los plátanos y córtelos en rebanadas de 1¼ centímetros. Póngalos en el agua salada. Sofría el tocino, escurra y tire la grasa. Pique el tocino y póngalo a un lado. Combine el ajo, aceite de oliva y sazón. Caliente el aceite de maíz y fría las rebanadas de plátano hasta que queden doradas. Escurra en toallas de papel. Mézclelos con unas gotas del aceite de ajo en un recipiente. Agregue ⅙ del tocino y 5 a 6 rebanadas de plátano. Machaque y presione firmemente en un mortero. Viértalo a un plato.

PARA EL PESTO DE CILANTRO:

2 tazas de cilantro
¾ taza de aceite de oliva
½ taza de queso Parmesano rallado
1 cucharadita de sazonador Cassave

2 cucharadas de jugo de limón
⅓ taza de nueces picadas
4 dientes de ajo
Pizca sal y pimienta

Combine todos los ingredientes en un procesador de alimentos y bata hasta que quede suave, pero con trocitos.

PARA LA SALSA CHIMICHURRI:

2 dientes de ajo
1 hoja de laurel
1 chile jalapeño, picado
½ cucharada de sal
⅛ taza de perejil finamente picado
⅛ taza de perejil (de hoja lisa) finamente picado

⅛ taza de cilantro finamente picado
2 cucharadas de sazonador "Jamaican Jerk"
¼ taza de aceite de oliva extra virgen
⅛ taza de vinagre blanco destilado

Mezcle todos los ingredientes para la salsa en un mortero hasta quedar hecha en una pasta suave (o se puede hacer puré en una batidora con un poco de vinagre). Transfiéralo a un recipiente y agregue el sazonador Jamaican Jerk. Bata todo, al mismo tiempo que añade el vinagre y aceite de oliva. Bátalo bien y póngalo a un lado. Divídalo a la mitad—una parte para la salsa y la otra para marinar las chuletas.

PARA LOS VEGETALES:

2 tazas de papas moradas, en cubitos	2 tazas de malanga, en cubitos
2 tazas de calabaza, en cubitos	1 cucharadita de aceite de oliva
2 tazas de chayote, en cubitos	1 cucharadita de ajo picado
2 tazas de apio, en cubitos	Sal y pimienta al gusto

Pase todos los vegetales por agua hirviendo durante un minuto y luego saltéelos en aceite de oliva con el ajo y sazone al gusto. Póngalos a un lado.

PARA SERVIR:

En una cacerola a prueba de horno, rápidamente ase el cordero por los dos lados. Póngalo en un horno precalentado a 425 grados F y rostice hasta que la carne llegue a una temperatura interna de 120 grados F, para medio término.

   Vierta el mofongo caliente al centro del plato templado. Ponga las chuletas recargadas hacia el mofongo. Decore el plato con los vegetales alrededor del plato, el pesto sobre las chuletas y las salsas en el plato. Termínelo con trozos de plátano.

SIRVE 4

GALETTES OF LOBSTER WITH TOMATO RISOTTO AND YUCCA

4 yuccas	1 teaspoon lobster base
Oil	1 cup Arborio rice
1 ounce onion, diced	1¼ cup fish stock
2 teaspoon garlic, chopped	½ cup dry white wine
2 ounces sun-dried tomatoes, finely sliced	Smoked Spanish cheese, shaved
12 (3-ounce) lobster tails, sliced in 4	(to taste)
1 ounce butter	2 tablespoons cilantro, chopped
1 tablespoon tomato paste	Salt and black pepper to taste

Trim each yucca to 2 to 2½ inches in diameter. Slice each yucca to the approximate thickness of a dime. Keep the slices together as you work. Brush two baking sheets with oil. On the baking sheets, arrange the slices from each yucca into circles 3 to 4 inches in diameter, overlapping them like shingles. Repeat with all four yucca, making 24 yucca galettes in all. Brush oil on top of the galettes and place in a 375-degree oven until they turn golden brown, 5 to 10 minutes. Remove from oven and let cool for 10 minutes.

   Sweat the onion, garlic, sun-dried tomatoes, and lobster tails in butter for 2 to 3 minutes. Remove lobster tails and set aside. Add the tomato paste and lobster base. Add the rice and mix thoroughly. Continue stirring until a toasted aroma develops.

   Add the stock in several additions, stirring the rice frequently (twice). Add the white wine and cook risotto until it is al dente and most of the liquid is absorbed. Add the lobster tails, cheese, and cilantro. Stir for a minute. The texture should be creamy.

FOR THE CILANTRO OIL:

2 tablespoons lime juice	Salt and black pepper to taste
2 tablespoons lemon juice	1 cup vegetable oil
½ cup cilantro, chopped	

Mix cilantro with citrus, blend in oil until emulsified, then season.

TO SERVE:

Place a yucca galette in the center of the plate. Add risotto on top. Repeat until you add the fourth galette. Garnish with shaved cheese on top. Drizzle cilantro oil around the plate.

LANGOSTA CON ARROZ AL TOMATE Y YUCA

4 yucas
Aceite
28 gramos cebolla, en cubitos
2 cucharaditas de ajo picado
56 gramos de tomates secados al sol, finamente rebanados
12 (84 gramos cada una) rabo de langostas
28 gramos de mantequilla

1 cucharada de tomate en pasta
1 cucharadita de caldo de langosta
1 taza de arroz Arborio
1¼ taza de caldo de pescado
½ taza de vino blanco seco
Queso Españole ahumado, rebanado finamente (al gusto)
2 cucharadas de cilantro picado
Sal y pimienta al gusto

Corte cada yuca para que tenga un diámetro de 5 a 6 centímetros. Rebane cada yuca al grosor aproximado de una moneda. Mantenga las rebanadas juntas mientras termina. Engrase dos placas para hornear con aceite. En las placas, arregle las rebanadas de yuca en círculos de 5 a 7½ centímetros de diámetro, poniéndolas una encima de la otra como si fueran tejas. Repita esto con las cuatro yucas, haciendo 24 círculos en total. Pase un poco de aceite sobre los círculos y póngalos en el horno a 375 grados hasta que estén dorados. Saque del horno y deje enfriar por 10 minutos.

Pase la cebolla, el ajo, los tomates secos y las langostas por mantequilla por 2 a 3 minutos. Saque las langostas y póngalas a un lado. Agregue el tomate en pasta y el caldo de langosta. Añada el arroz y mezcle completamente. Continúe moviendo hasta obtener un aroma a tostado.

Añada el caldo en varias adiciones, moviendo el arroz dos veces. Agregue el vino blanco y cocine el arroz hasta que esté al dente y se haya absorbido todo el líquido. Agregue las langostas, el queso y cilantro. Mueva un minuto. La textura deberá ser cremosa.

PARA EL ACEITE DE CILANTRO:

2 cucharadas de jugo de lima
2 cucharadas de jugo de limón
½ taza de cilantro, picado

Sal y pimienta al gusto
1 taza de aceite vegetal

Mezclar el cilantro con el jugo cítrico, mezclar con el aceite hasta que se haya emulsificado y sazonar.

PARA SERVIR:

Ponga uno de los círculos de yuca en el centro del plato. Agregue el arroz encima. Repita hasta que haya puesta el cuarto círculo. Decore con los quesos encima. Ponga un poquito de aceite de cilantro alrededor del plato.

Suzana Davila

CHICKEN IN MOLE VERDE

Cooking oil
6 corn tortillas
1 cup sesame seeds
½ cup hulled raw pumpkin seeds
⅓ cup natural pistachio nuts, shelled
⅓ cup whole almonds, blanched
3 poblano chili peppers, chopped
4 serrano chili peppers, chopped
1½ cups tomatillos, chopped and husked
    (about ½ pound)

1 large bunch fresh cilantro (about 2 cups
    packed)
1 cup iceberg lettuce, shredded
4 large cloves garlic
4 cups chicken broth
3 tablespoons cooking oil
2 pounds cooked chicken (or turkey or
    pork), cut into strips

Heat ¼ inch cooking oil in a large, heavy skillet over moderately high heat. Fry tortillas one at a time until golden brown on both sides. Drain on paper towels. Cool tortillas and break into pieces.

Toast sesame seeds in a dry 10- to 12-inch heavy skillet over moderate heat about 8 minutes or until golden brown, stirring frequently; transfer to a bowl to cool. Add pumpkin seeds to skillet; stirring frequently, toast 2 to 3 minutes or until they puff up but do not darken. Transfer pumpkin seeds to bowl with sesame seeds. Add pistachio nuts and almonds to skillet and toast 2 to 3 minutes or until golden brown. Transfer nuts to bowl with seed mixture; cool.

Place tortilla pieces, chili peppers, tomatillos, cilantro, lettuce, garlic, and 1½ to 2 cups of the broth in a food processor. Cover and process untill mixture forms a thick paste. Add seed-nut mixture and process until sauce is well combined but not smooth.

Heat the 3 tablespoons oil in a large saucepan over moderate heat; add sauce. Cook over medium heat about 12 minutes, stirring frequently. Add remaining broth as needed to reach a thick, pasty consistency.

Stir in chicken, turkey, or pork and cook mixture for 10 minutes, stirring frequently.

SERVES 6 TO 8

POLLO EN MOLE VERDE

Aceite para cocinar
6 tortillas de maíz
1 taza ajonjolí
½ taza de semillas de calabaza
   sin cáscara
⅓ taza almendras sin cáscara
⅓ taza alfóncigos sin cáscara
3 chiles poblanos, picados
4 chiles serranos, picados

1½ tazas de tomatillos cortados
   (más o menos 150 gramos)
1 manojo de cilantro fresco (2 tazas)
1 taza de lechuga iceberg cortada
4 dientes grandes de ajo
4 tazas caldo de pollo
3 cucharadas aceite de cocina
1 kilogramo de pollo cocido (o pavo o
   cerdo), cortado en tiras

Caliente ⅗ centímetros de aceite en un sartén grande a fuego moderadamente alto hasta que esté caliente. Fría las tortillas una a la vez hasta que estén doradas por los dos lados. Escárralas en toallitas de papel. Enfríe las tortillas y rómpalas en pedacitos.

Tueste el ajonjolí en un sartén de 25 a 30 centímetros, seco, a fuego moderado por 8 minutos o hasta quedar dorado, moviendo frecuentemente. Páselas a un plato para que se enfríen. Agregue las semillas de calabaza al sartén, moviendo constantemente, tuéstelas por 2 a 3 minutos o hasta que se hinchen, pero que no se oscurezcan. Ponga las semillas de calabaza junto con el ajonjolí. Ponga los alfóncigos y almendras en el sartén y tueste por 2 a 3 minutos o hasta que estén dorados. Póngalos con las demás semillas; enfríe.

Ponga los trozos de tortilla, chiles, tomatillos, cilantro, lechuga, ajo y 1½ a 2 tazas del caldo en un procesador de alimentos. Cubra y muélalo hasta que se forme una pasta espesa. Agregue la mezcla de semillas y nueces y muela hasta que la salsa se combine bien, pero no esté lisa.

Caliente las 3 cucharadas de aceite en un sartén grande a fuego moderado hasta que esté caliente; agregue la salsa. Cocine a fuego medio por más o menos 12 minutos, moviendo frecuentemente. Agregue el resto del caldo si es necesario para adquirir una consistencia espesa.

Agregue el pollo, pavo o cerdo y cocine la mezcla por 10 minutes, moviendo frecuentemente.

SIRVE 6 A 8

POLLO PICADILLO-STUFFED PEPPERS

4 whole medium-sized chicken breasts
(about 4 pounds)
1 medium carrot, cut up
1 medium onion, cut up
1 large Roma tomato, halved
1 tablespoon chicken base or instant
chicken bouillon granules
3 bay leaves
2 whole black peppercorns
1 medium onion, cut into thin wedges
6 cloves garlic, minced

2 tablespoons olive oil
3 large Roma tomatoes, cut into thin
wedges
1 cup snipped fresh cilantro
3/4 cup green olives, sliced
1/4 cup raisins
3 green onions, thinly sliced
4 teaspoons dried Mexican oregano
or regular dried oregano, crushed
1/2 teaspoon ground black pepper
8 poblano chili peppers, roasted

Remove and discard skin from chicken breasts. Place chicken in a very large saucepan or Dutch oven; add enough water to cover (about 5 cups). Add the carrot, onion, the halved tomato, chicken base or bouillon granules, bay leaves, and peppercorns. Bring to a boil. Reduce heat and simmer, covered, 25 to 30 minutes or until chicken is tender. Remove chicken, reserving broth; set chicken aside until cool enough to handle. Discard solids from broth. Remove chicken from bones and cut into strips, discarding bones.

Cook onion wedges and garlic in hot olive oil in a large skillet until tender. Add tomato wedges, cilantro, olives, raisins, green onions, oregano, black pepper, and 1/2 cup of the reserved chicken broth. Stir in chicken. Cover and cook over low heat for 5 to 10 minutes, or until it is heated through and flavors are blended, stirring once or twice.

Cut a slit in the side of each chili pepper, leaving stem attached; remove seeds and ribs. Spoon chicken mixture into each pepper. Serve at once.

SERVES 8

CHILES RELLENOS DE PICADILLO DE POLLO

4 pechugas medianas enteras de pollo
(más o menos 2 kilogramos)
1 zanahoria mediana, cortada
1 cebolla mediana, cortada
1 tomate Roma grande, a la mitad
1 cucharada de caldo de pollo (natural
instantáneo)
3 hojas de laurel
2 granos de pimienta
1 cebolla mediana, cortada en rodajas
finas
6 dientes de ajo, picados

2 cucharadas de aceite de oliva
3 tomates Roma grandes, cortados en
rodajas finas
1 taza cilantro, despuntado
¾ taza aceitunas verdes, en rebanadas
¼ taza pasas
3 cebollitas verdes, finamente cortadas
4 cucharaditas orégano seco Mexicano,
machacado
½ cucharadita de pimienta negra molida
8 chiles poblanos, rostizados

Quite y deseche la piel del pollo. Ponga el pollo en una olla grande. Agregue suficiente agua para cubrir todo (5 tazas más o menos). Agregue la zanahoria, la cebolla cortada, el tomate cortado a la mitad, el caldo de pollo, las hojas de laurel y los granos de pimientas. Déjelo hervir. Reduzca la llama y deje hervir, cubierto, 25 a 30 minutos o hasta que el pollo esté blando. Saque el pollo, guarde el caldo; deje enfriar el pollo. Saque las partes sálidas del caldo. Quite la carne de los huesos y córtela en tiras, desechando los huesos.

Cocine las rodajas de cebolla y el ajo en aceite de oliva caliente en un sartén hasta que estén blandos. Añada las rodajas de tomate, el cilantro, aceitunas, pasas, cebollitas, orégano, pimienta y ½ taza del caldo. Añada el pollo. Cúbralo y cocínelo a fuego bajo por 5 a 10 minutos o hasta que se haya calentado bien y los sabores se hayan mezclado, moviendo una o dos veces.

Haga una cortada al lado de cada chile, dejándoles el tallo; quite las semillas. Con una cuchara ponga la mezcla del pollo dentro de cada chile. Sirva inmediatamente.

SIRVE 8

Oscar de la Hoya

CALABACITAS COLACHE (ZUCCHINI COLACHE)

¼ cup vegetable oil
1 tomato, diced
1 onion, chopped
4 or 5 zucchini, sliced

1 teaspoon salt (or to taste)
1 teaspoon black pepper (or to taste)
1 can (16 ounces) whole corn, drained
½ pound grated Monterey Jack cheese

Heat oil in a skillet over medium heat. Add the tomato and onion. Sauté for approximately 2 minutes. Next, add the zucchini, salt, and pepper. Cover and allow to simmer over low heat. After approximately 10 minutes or when tender, add the corn. Simmer for 5 minutes. Add cheese and cover until cheese is fully melted.

SERVES 4

¼ taza aceite vegetal
1 tomate, cortado
1 cebolla, cortada
4 o 5 calabacitas, picadas

1 cucharita sal (o al gusto)
1 cucharita pimienta (o al gusto)
1 lata maíz entero (colada)
250 gramos queso "Monterey Jack," rallado

Calienta el aceite en un sartén sobre un fuego medio. Añadir los tomates y cebollas cortadas. Cocinar por dos minutos. Luego, añadir las calabacitas, sal y pimienta (al gusto). Cocinar sobre fuego lento y tapar. Después de 10 minutos, añadir el maíz. Sigue cocinando sobre fuego lento por 5 minutos. Añadir el queso rallado, tapar hasta que el queso se derrita.

SIRVE 4

EMPANADAS DE LIMÓN

3 egg yolks
½ pound butter, softened
2 teaspoons baking powder
¼ pound lard or Crisco shortening
½ teaspoon salt
½ pound granulated sugar
1½ pounds flour
1 cup milk
1 jar lemon jelly
     (can substitute jelly of choice)

In a large mixing bowl, add egg yolks, butter, baking powder, lard or shortening, salt, and sugar. Mix well. Add flour. Mix well. Add milk and mix again until soft, then form dough into the shape of a small tortilla (about ¼-inch thick). Place a tablespoon of lemon jelly (or substitute) in the center of each shape. Fold over and place on a nonstick baking sheet. Bake at 350 degrees for 15 minutes or until golden brown. Allow to cool and serve.

MAKES 12 EMPANADAS

---

3 yemas de huevo
228 gramos mantequilla (suavizada)
2 cucharitas polvo para hornear
114 gramos manteca o Crisco
½ cucharita sal
228 gramos azúcar
680 gramos harina
1 taza leche
1 frasco marmelada de limón (sustituya
     la mermelada que quiera)

En un cuenco grande, mezcla las yemas de huevos, mantequilla, polvos para hornear, manteca, sal y azúcar. Añadir la harina y mezclar de nuevo. Añadir la leche y mezclar otra vez hasta que esté suave y ponga la masa en forma de una tortilla. Ponga una cucharada de marmelada en el centro de cada tortilla. Doblar y poner en el horno de 350 grados por 15 minutos o hasta que estén doradas. Retirar del horno y servir.

HACE 12 EMPANADAS

CHILAQUILES

1½ pounds corn tortillas
1 cup vegetable oil
1 tomato, diced
2 fresh jalapeño peppers, finely chopped
  (only if you like it spicy)

1 teaspoon onion, chopped
1 teaspoon salt
1 cup tomato sauce
4 eggs, lightly beaten
½ pound grated Monterey Jack cheese

Cut tortillas into square pieces. Heat the oil in a large skillet and sauté tortilla squares over medium heat until they are lightly browned and slightly crispy. Drain and discard excess oil. Over medium heat, add the tomato, jalapeños, onion, and salt to the tortillas and cook for about 3 minutes. Next, pour tomato sauce and eggs over tortilla mixture. Stir constantly until eggs are firm. Sprinkle grated cheese over eggs, and continue cooking until cheese melts.

SERVES 4

---

680 gramos tortillas de maíz
1 taza aceite de vegetal
1 tomate, cortado
2 jalapeño frescos, cortados finamente
  (solo si te gusta picoso)

1 cucharita cebolla, picada
1 cucharita sal
1 taza salsa de tomate
4 huevos, batidos ligeramente
228 gramos queso "Monterey Jack," rallado

Corta las tortillas en pedazos cuadrados. Sobre un fuego medio, calienta el aceite en un sartén grande, y cocina las tortillas hasta que se pongan duras. Colar el aceite que quede. Añadir el tomate, jalapeños, cebollas, y sal a las tortillas y cocinar por 3 minutos. Luego, añadir la salsa de tomate y huevos sobre la mezcla de tortillas. Mezclar constantemente hasta que los huevos se pongan firmes. Agregar el queso y continuar cocinando hasta que el queso se derrita.

SIRVE 4

TALLOTAS RELLENAS (STUFFED TALLOTAS)

6 tallotas
½ cup mayonnaise
2 eggs
1 teaspoon salt

1 teaspoon curry powder
1 teaspoon pepper
1 teaspoon sugar
2 tablespoons grated Parmesan cheese

Cut the tallotas in half. Put them in a pot of boiling water for a half hour. When they are soft, take them out of the water. Let them cool and then, with a spoon, remove the pulp. Add pulp to all the remaining ingredients, except the Parmesan cheese, and puree in a blender or food processor. Season to taste. Put the puree mix inside the skin and sprinkle with the cheese. Bake in a 350-degree oven until golden in color.

SERVES 6

Oscar de la Renta

HERE ARE TWO OF MY FAVORITE RECIPES—ONE THAT WE COOK IN THE DOMINICAN REPUBLIC, MY HOMELAND, AND ONE THAT WE COOK IN THE UNITED STATES.

I HOPE YOU ENJOY THEM...

6 tallotas
½ taza mayonesa
2 huevos
1 cucharita sal

1 cucharita polvo de curry
1 cucharita pimienta
1 cucharita azúcar
2 cucharadas queso Parmesano

Corta las tallotas por la mitad. Ponga a hervir por media hora. Cuando estén suaves, remover de la agua. Dejar enfriar y remover la pulpa con una cuchara. Añadir la pulpa con el resto de los ingredientes para hacer un puré. Sazonar a gusto. Poner la mezcla dentro de las tallotas y poner queso encima. Poner en el horno a 350 grados para cocinar.

SIRVE 6

SOPA DE CALABAZAS Y CANGREJO (PUMPKIN AND CRAB SOUP)

1 medium pumpkin
4 scallions, white part only, minced
½ teaspoon coriander
6 cups chicken consomme
2 tablespoon curry powder
½ teaspoon cinnamon
½ teaspoon brown sugar

1 tablespoon olive oil
Salt to taste
Black pepper to taste
2 ears fresh corn
1 pound lump crabmeat
2 cups fresh plain yogurt

Cutting horizontally, remove top of pumpkin, then scoop out all of the flesh from inside. Remove seeds and strings from pumpkin flesh and set aside. Place top back on the pumpkin shell and put in a 250-degree oven for a couple of hours or until the skin takes on a deeper golden color. The pumpkin shell will be used as the soup tureen.

In a blender or food processor, puree the pumpkin flesh, scallions, and coriander. Place the consomme in a large pot over medium heat and bring to a simmer. Add the curry powder, cinnamon, brown sugar, olive oil, and salt and pepper. Bring to a simmer again. Cut uncooked kernels from corn cobs (corn must be very fresh, young, and tender). Add corn and crabmeat to mixture. Before serving, add yogurt and stir, then transfer to the pumpkin shell.

SERVES 4

1 calabaza mediana
4 cebollas verdes, parte blanca
   solamente, cortada
½ cucharita cilantro
6 tazas consomé de pollo
2 cucharadas polvo de curry
½ cucharita canela

½ cucharita azúcar moreno
1 cucharada aceite de oliva
Sal (al gusto)
Pimienta (al gusto)
2 mazorcas de maíz frescas
454 gramos carne de cangrejo
2 tazas yogurt natural (sin sabor) fresco

Cortando horizontalmente, remover la tapa de la calabaza, sacar la pulpa, remover las semillas, y poner a un lado. Colocar la tapa de la calabaza de nuevo y poner en un horno de 250 grados por dos horas. La calabaza será tu cazuela para servir la sopa.

En una batidora, mezclar la pulpa de la calabaza, el cilantro, y las cebollas verdes. Ponga a hervir el consomé en un sartén sobre fuego medio. Añadir el polvo de curry, canela, azúcar moreno, aceite de oliva, sal y pimienta. Hervir de nuevo. Corta el maíz crudo (que esté muy fresco y tierno) y añadir con la carne de cangrejo. Antes de servir, añadir el yogurt y mezclar.

SIRVE 4

MUSSEL SOUP WITH CILANTRO AND SERRANO CHILI

FOR THE CILANTRO PUREE:

4 large bunches of cilantro, roughly chopped

½ bunch parsley, roughly chopped

¼ yellow onion, roughly chopped

2 cloves garlic, roughly chopped

2 serrano chilies, stems removed

½ cup fish stock

Place the first five ingredients in a blender and puree with just enough fish stock to form a very thick and smooth puree.

FOR THE ANCHO CHILI JAM:

1 pound ancho peppers

2 tablespoons vinegar

¼ cup honey

3 ounces red currant jelly

1 shallot

1 clove garlic

½ teaspoon salt

Soak ancho peppers in warm water until very soft. Drain off the water and puree the chilies in a blender with the vinegar, honey, jelly, shallot, and garlic. Continue to puree until very smooth and thick. Adjust honey or vinegar to balance spiciness and tartness/sweetness.

PREPARING THE SOUP:

60 mussels, cleaned

1 cup fish stock

3 cups cream

Cilantro serrano puree

Cilantro leaves

Place the mussels in a small soup pot with the fish stock. Cover and bring to a boil. Steam the mussels until the shells are just opened. Remove the mussels from the pan and remove the mussels from the shells. Boil the liquid again in the pot to reduce it to approximately 1 cup. Add the cream to the stock and boil again until the liquid is slightly thickened. Add enough cilantro puree to the pot to thicken the soup. Bring the liquid to a boil for a few seconds. Place the warm mussels into six soup bowls. Pour the hot soup over the mussels. Fill one mussel shell with Ancho Chili Jam and lay the shell on top of the mussels so that it does not sink into the soup. Garnish with cilantro leaves and serve.

SERVES 6

Robert del Grande

ROBERT DEL GRANDE IS ONE OF THE MOST CELEBRATED CHEFS IN AMERICA AND IS CHEF/PARTNER IN ONE OF THE MOST ADMIRED RESTAURANTS IN AMERICA, CAFÉ ANNIE IN HOUSTON, TEXAS. ROBERT IS ALSO A PARTNER IN CAFÉ EXPRESS, A SPORTY TAKE-OUT "GOOD FOOD FAST" CAFÉ WITH FIVE LOCATIONS IN HOUSTON AND ONE IN DALLAS, AS WELL AS IN RIO RANCH, WITH ITS COWBOY CUISINE.

ROBERT WAS BORN IN 1954 AND RECEIVED HIS B.S. IN CHEMISTRY AND BIOLOGY FROM THE UNIVERSITY OF SAN FRANCISCO AND A PH.D. IN BIOCHEMISTRY FROM THE UNIVERSITY OF CALIFORNIA, RIVERSIDE. HE BEGAN EXPERIMENTING IN THE KITCHEN AT CAFÉ ANNIE IN 1981 WHEN HE CAME TO HOUSTON TO VISIT HIS NOW-WIFE, MIMI. HE REMAINED IN HOUSTON AND BECAME EXECUTIVE CHEF AT CAFÉ ANNIE, WHERE HE DEVELOPED HIS AMERICAN COOKING WITH A SOUTHWESTERN EDGE. HE HAS

SOPA DE MEJILLONES CON CILANTRO Y CHILE SERRANO

PARA EL PURÉ DE CILANTRO:

4 manojos de cilantro, picados en grueso
½ manojo de perejil, picados en grueso
¼ cebolla amarilla, picada en grueso

2 dientes de ajo, machacado
2 chiles serranos (sin el pedúnculo)
½ taza consomé de pescado

Coloque los primeros 5 ingredientes en la batidora y haga puré con solamente suficiciente consomé de pollo hasta formar un puré de consistencia espesa.

PARA EL CHILE ANCHO:

454 gramos chiles anchos
2 cucharadas vinagre
¼ taza miel
84 gramos jalea de arándanos rojos

1 cebollita verde
1 diente de ajo
½ cucharadita sal

Remojar el chile ancho en agua tibia hasta que esté suave. Quite el agua y haga los chiles puré en la batidora, con el vinagre, miel, jalea, cebollita y ajo. Continúe haciendo el puré hasta que se vea suave y denso. Ajuste la miel o el vinagre para balancear las especies y dulzura.

PREPARANDO LA SOPA:

60 mejillones, lavados
1 taza consomé de pescado
3 tazas crema

Puré de chile serrano y cilantro
Hojas de cilantro

Coloque los mejillones en un pequeña olla con el consomé de pescado. Hágalo hervir por unos minutos hasta que vea abrir la conchas. Sáque las almejas de sus conchas. Hierva el caldillo de la olla hasta que el líquido quede reducido a una taza. Agregue la crema hasta que se haga espeso. Agregue el puré de cilantro en la cazuela hasta que la sopa se vea espesa. Caliente hasta punto de ebullición por unos segundos. Ponga los mejillones calientes en el fondo de un plato hondo. Agregue la sopa caliente y espesa sobre los mejillones. Llene uno de los mejillones con jalea de chile ancho y ponga la cáscara de éste mejillón sobre los mejillones de tal forma de que no se unda en la sopa. Adorne con hojas de cilantro y sirva

SIRVE 6

Robert del Grande

RECEIVED NUMEROUS CULINARY AWARDS AND HONORS, INCLUDING THE JAMES BEARD AWARD, 1992; IVY AWARD, 1992 (*RESTAURANT AND INSTITUTIONS MAGAZINE*); DISTINGUISHED RESTAURANTS AWARD, 1992 (*CONDÉ NAST TRAVELER*); DISTINGUISHED RESTAURANTS OF NORTH AMERICA, 1992 (DIRONA AWARD); FINE DINING HALL OF FAME (*NATION'S RESTAURANT NEWS*); WHO'S WHO OF COOKING IN AMERICA (*COOK'S MAGAZINE*); WHO'S WHO OF COOKING IN TEXAS; AND HONOR ROLL OF AMERICAN CHEFS (*FOOD & WINE* MAGAZINE). ROBERT WAS FEATURED IN THE PBS *GREAT CHEFS* SERIES WITH PIERRE FRANEY IN 1992 AND ALSO APPEARED IN THE 1994 PRODUCTION *COOKING WITH MASTER CHEFS* FEATURING JULIA CHILD.

HE HAS BEEN FEATURED IN SUCH PUBLICATIONS AS *COOKING WITH MASTER CHEFS* BY JULIA CHILD; *FOOD & WINE*, JANUARY 1994; *WINE SPECTATOR*, DECEMBER 1993; *GOURMET*, APRIL 1993; *CONDÉ NAST TRAVELER*, JANUARY 1990, 1991, 1992, 1993; *SELF*, JUNE 1992; *ELLE*, APRIL 1991, MARCH 1992; *COOKING LIGHT*, MARCH/APRIL 1991; *ESQUIRE*, NOVEMBER 1990, JANUARY 1994; *W*, SEPTEMBER 1990; *NEW YORK TIMES*, JULY 1990; *MIRABELLA*, NOVEMBER 1990; *BON APPETIT*, FEBRUARY 1990, APRIL 1993; AND *RESTAURANT HOSPITALITY* (COVER), MARCH 1993.

Robert del Grande

CRAB TOSTADAS WITH AVOCADO RELISH AND SALSA

FOR THE CRABMEAT:

12 ounces fresh lump crabmeat
2 tablespoons heavy cream

1 teaspoon mayonnaise

Pick through the crabmeat to be sure it is free of any shells. In a mixing bowl, combine the cream and the mayonnaise and blend until smooth. Add the crabmeat and mix to coat. Do not overwork the mixture. The crabmeat should not become too finely shredded.

FOR THE CABBAGE SALAD:

¼ head white cabbage
¼ cup sour cream
1 tablespoon lime juice

2 small serrano chilies, seeded
   and finely chopped
Salt and black pepper

Very finely slice the cabbage (chiffonade). Blend the sour cream, lime juice, and chilies in a bowl until smooth. Add the cabbage and mix until the cabbage is coated with the sour cream. Add salt and pepper to taste.

FOR THE AVOCADO RELISH:

2 ripe California avocados (8 ounces each)
½ red bell pepper, finely chopped (4
   ounces, about ½ cup)
1 small red onion, finely chopped (6
   ounces, about 1 cup)
2 serrano chilies (may substitute
   jalapeños), minced (1 tablespoon)

1 bunch cilantro, chopped (4 ounces,
   about ¾ cup), reserve some leaves
   for garnish
2 tablespoons hazelnut oil
1 lime (2 tablespoons juice)
Salt and black pepper

Split and seed the avocados. Remove the skins. Cut the avocados into very small cubes. In a mixing bowl, combine the avocado, bell pepper, onion, chilies, cilantro, hazelnut oil, and lime juice. Thoroughly mix the ingredients to form a coarse relish. Add salt and pepper to taste.

FOR THE TOMATO SALSA:

6 ripe plum tomatoes, chopped (1 pound,
   about 2 cups)
½ red onion, minced (½ cup)
1 bunch cilantro, chopped (¾ cup), reserve
   some leaves for garnish

1 serrano chili (may substitute jalapeño),
   minced (2 teaspoons)
1 lime (2 tablespoons juice)
Salt and black pepper

Combine the tomatoes with the onion, cilantro, and chili. Add the lime juice and mix thoroughly. Add salt and pepper to taste.

FOR THE TORTILLAS:
8 small white corn tortillas
¼ cup oil

Prepare 8 fresh tortillas that are approximately 3 inches in diameter, or cut 3-inch tortilla rounds from commercially available white corn tortillas. In a small skillet, heat oil until very hot. Fry the tortillas until golden brown and crisp.

ASSEMBLING THE TOSTADAS:
Spread some of the cabbage mixture on each crisp tortilla. Layer the avocado relish over the cabbage. Place crabmeat on the avocado relish and top with the tomato salsa. Garnish the tostadas with cilantro leaves.

SERVES 4

TOSTADAS DE CANGREJO CON SALSA DE AGUACATE CON RÁBANO

PARA LA CARNE DE CANGREJO:
336 gramos carne fresca de cangrejo
2 cucharadas crema condensada (nata líquida)
1 cucharita mayonesa

Revise la carne de cangrejo para asegurarse de que no tiene pedazos de concha. En una olla combine la crema y la mayonesa y bata hasta que esté suave. Agregue la carne de cangrejo y mezcle hasta que cubra la cangre de cangrejo. No mezcle de más, la carne de cangrejo no debe estar muy finamente deshebrada.

PARA LA ENSALADA DE REPOLLO:
¼ cabeza repollo blanco
¼ taza crema agria
1 cucharada jugo de lima
2 chiles serranos pequeños, con semilla y finamente picados
Sal y pimienta

Finamente corte el repollo. Mezcle la crema agria, jugo de lima y pique los chiles en un recipiente hasta que estén finitos. Agregue el repollo y mezcle hasta que el repollo esté cubierto con crema agria. Agregue sal y pimienta al gusto.

Robert del Grande

PARA EL AGUACATE ARRABANADO:

2 aguacates California maduros,
    228 gramos cada uno
½ chile pimiento rojo, finamente picados
    (112 gramos, ½ taza)
1 cebolla roja chica, finamente picada
    (168 gramos, 1 taza)
2 chiles serranos machacados (una
    cucharada, o jalapeños)

1 manojo cilantro machacado
    (112 gramos, ¾ de taza)
2 cucharadas aceite de avellanas
1 lima (2 cucharadas de jugo)
Sal y pimienta

Corte los aguacates por la mitad, quíteles la cáscara. Corte los aguacates en pequeños cubos. En una olla de mezclar, combiné los aguacates cortados, pimiento rojo, cebolla roja, chile serrano, cilantro, aceite de avellanas y jugo de lima. Mezcle bién todos los ingredientes, formando una masa gruesa. Sal y pimienta al gusto.

PARA LA SALSA DE TOMATE:

6 tomates maduros, picados (455 gramos,
    como dos tazas)
½ cebolla roja, machacada (½ taza)
1 manojo cilantro, machacado y guarde
    una hojas para decorar

1 chile serrano o jalapeño machacado,
    (como 2 cucharadas)
1 lima (2 cucharadas de jugo)
Sal y pimienta

Pique fínamente los tomates. Combine con la cebolla, cilantro y chile. Agregue el jugo de la lima y mezcle bien. Sal y pimienta al gusto.

LAS TORTILLAS:

8 tortillas pequeñas de maíz blanco
¼ taza aceite

Prepare 8 tortillas de maíz de aproximadamente 7½ centímetros de diámetro, o corte círculos de tortila de 7½ centímetros de diámetro. En un sartén, caliente un cuarto de taza de aceite hasta que esté bién caliente. Fría las tortillas hasta que estén doradas y crujientes.

ENSAMBLANDO LAS TOSTADAS:

Esparza la mezcla de repollo en la tortilla. Ponga en capas la mezcla de aguacate. Agregue un poco de carne de cangrejo en el aguacate y encima agregue la salsa de tomate. Adorne con las hojas de cilantro.

SIRVE 4

ARROZ CON GRANDULES

1 pound pork, cut into chunks
2 spicy red peppers, chopped
3 packages sofrito
½ cup chopped ham
2 envelopes Sazon seasoning with achiote

2 beef bouillon cubes
3½ cups water
1 large can (16 ounces) fresh grandules
9 spicy olives
2 cups rice

In a large pot over medium heat, sauté the pork, peppers, sofrito, and ham for several minutes. Add water along with the seasoning and bouillon and bring to a boil. Add the grandules, olives, and rice. When the water begins to evaporate, reduce heat to low, cover, and stir occasionally until done.

SERVES 6

---

454 gramos carne picada de cerdo
2 ajíes rojos picoso (cortados)
3 paquetes sofrito
½ taza jamón cortado
2 sobres Sazón con achiote

2 cubitos de consome de carne
3½ tazas agua
1 lata (454 gramos) grandules frescos
9 aceitunas picosas
2 tazas arroz

En un sartén grande sobre fuego mediano, cocina el cerdo, ajíes, sofrito, y el jamón por 6 a 8 minutos. Añadir la agua con el sazón y el consomé y poner a hervir. Añadir el arroz, aceitunas y grandules. Cuando el agua se comienza a evaporar, ponga sobre fuego lento, tapar, y mezclar hasta que este hecho.

SIRVE 6

Michael DeLorenzo

THIS IS MY FAVORITE RECIPE BECAUSE IT REMINDS ME OF HOME AND WHERE I CAME FROM. IT'S ALSO DELICIOUS. THE AROMA WILL HELP YOU CREATE YOUR OWN MEMORIES.

Placido Domingo

PAELLA DOMINGO

1 chicken (2 to 3 pounds)
1 carrot, chopped
1 onion, quartered
1 stalk celery, chopped
2 bay leaves
½ pound mussels
8 ounces pork, diced
4 large shrimp, shell on
3 ounces olive oil (divided use)
½ Spanish onion, diced
1 tomato, diced
4 ounces Spanish chorizo
Salt and black pepper to taste
1 pound rice (Bomba, Calasparra)
Pinch saffron
1 clove garlic, ground
Juice of ½ lemon
4 ounces fresh peas
1 roasted pepper, sliced
Parsley for garnish

Clean and trim the chicken of fat and cut into even pieces, then place in a stock pot and cover with water, adding carrot, onion, celery, and bay leaves. Cook until chicken is tender. Strain and reserve the chicken and broth. Discard the vegetables.

Debeard and clean the mussels and place in a stock pot; cover ⅓ with water and bring to a simmer. When the mussels open, strain and reserve the liquid. Remove top shell and reserve mussels. Cut pork into small pieces and clean the shrimp, but keep the shells on.

In a skillet over medium heat, heat half the olive oil and add the onion; sauté until soft; add the tomato and pork and stir. Cover and cook 5 to 8 minutes, then add chicken and chorizo and cook, covered, for another minute. Take off heat.

In a saucepan over high heat, mix chicken and mussel stocks and bring to a boil. Keep simmering and add salt to taste.

In a paella pan over medium heat, add the other half of the olive oil and heat to medium. Sauté the rice until well coated and crisp. Add the vegetables and chicken and stir into the rice. Add the stock, saffron, salt, pepper, and garlic (shake the pan to distribute the spices).

Bring to a simmer and don't stir again. Cook for 10 minutes, then add the lemon juice, shrimp, mussels, and peas. Place the sliced pepper on top. Cook for 5 more minutes. The rice will absorb all the broth.

NOTE: For 1 cup of rice (makes 2 portions) use 2½ cups of broth. If the paella is getting a bit dry, add extra broth before the end. It is important to taste the paella constantly in order to reach the right consistency.

SERVES 4

PAELLA DOMINGO

1 pollo (1 kilogramo)
1 zanahoria, cortada
1 cebolla, cortada
1 apio, cortado
2 hojas de laurel
228 gramos mejillones
228 gramos cerdo, cortado
4 camarones grandes, con cáscara
100 gramos aceite de oliva
½ cebolla Española, cortada

1 tomate, cortado
112 gramos chorizo Español
Sal y pimienta (al gusto)
454 gramos arroz (Bomba, Calasparra)
Pizca azafrán
1 diente de ajo, machacado
Jugo de ½ limón
112 gramos guisantes
1 ají, a sado y rebanado
Perejil para adorno

Limpie el pollo y cortar en pedazos iguales. Ponga a cocinar en una cazuela honda cubierta con agua, zanahoria, cebollas, apio, y hoja de laurel. Cocinar hasta que el pollo esté blando. Colar y reservar el pollo y el agua. Sacar los vegetales.

Limpiar los mejillones y poner en un sartén hondo con ⅓ de agua y ponga a hervir. Cuando los mejillones comiencen a abrir, colar y reservar el agua. Sacar los mejillones de la concha y reservar. Cortar el cerdo en pedazos pequeños y limpiar los camarones, pero dejarlos en su cáscara.

En un sartén sobre fuego mediano, calentar la mitad de aciete de oliva y añadir la cebolla. Cocinar hasta que esté blanda. Añadir los tomates, cerdo, y mezclar. Tapar y cocinar por 5 a 8 minutos, añadir el pollo y chorizo y cocinar, tapado, por otro minuto. Remover del fuego.

En un sartén sobre fuego alto, mezclar el jugo del pollo y mejillones y poner a hervir, añadir sal a gusto.

En una paellera, sobre fuego mediano, añadir la otra mitad del aceite de oliva y cocinar sobre fuego mediano. Mezclar el arroz. Añadir los vegetales y pollo y mezclar el arroz. Añadir los caldos y azafrán, sal, pimienta, y ajo (mezclar la cazuela para esparcir las especias).

Hervir de nuevo y no mezclar más. Cocinar por 15 minutos, 5 minutos antes de que termine, añadir el jugo de limón, los camarones y mejillones encima, con los guisantes y ajíes. Cocinar por 5 minutos más. El arroz absorberá el caldo.

NOTA: Para ½ taza de arroz (2 porciones) se necesita 2½ tazas de caldo. Si la paella empieza a resecarse, puede agregar un poco más de caldo. Es importante probarla constantemante para obtener la consistencia correcta.

SIRVE 4

Hector Elizondo

ASOPAO DE CIDRA

3 to 3½ pounds chicken, cut into pieces
4 to 5 tablespoons olive oil
4 or 5 cloves garlic, minced
1 large onion, chopped
2 stalks celery, chopped
1 large carrot, chopped
1 red bell pepper, chopped
1¼ cups long grain rice, brown or white
1 cup dry white wine or dry vermouth
4 or 5 plum tomatoes, chopped

2 tablespoons capers
½ cup small green olives with pimiento
1 teaspoon dried oregano, or to taste
2 or 3 bay leaves
Dash cayenne pepper, or to taste
Salt and black pepper to taste
3 cups chicken broth, fresh or canned
1 cup water
1 package frozen grandules
Handful cilantro or parsley, chopped

Wash and dry the chicken pieces, removing unwanted fat. In a pot over medium heat, sauté chicken in olive oil, turning until brown. Remove from pot. Add garlic, onion, celery, carrot, and bell pepper. Sauté 3 to 4 minutes. Add rice and stir until rice becomes translucent and aromatic. Return chicken to pot and add the wine or vermouth, stirring well. Add the tomatoes, capers, olives, spices, chicken broth, and water. Bring to a boil and simmer until rice is cooked, adding more chicken broth if necessary. This dish should be quite soupy. When rice is nearly cooked, add grandules. Just before serving, stir in the cilantro or parsley.

SERVES 6

---

1 a 1½ kilogramos pollo, cortado en pedazos
4 a 5 cucharas aceite de oliva
4 o 5 dientes de ajo, cortado
1 cebolla grande, cortada
2 apios, cortado
1 zanahória grande, cortada
1 aji rojo, cortado
1¼ tazas arroz de largo grano
1 taza vino blanco seco o vermut seco
4 a 5 tomates pequeños, cortado

2 cucharadas alcaparras
½ taza aceitunas verdes con pimiento
1 cucharita orégano seco (o al gusto)
2 o 3 hojas de laurel
Pizca pimentón (o al gusto)
Sal y pimienta (al gusto)
3 tazas caldo de pollo, fresco o de lata
1 taza agua
1 paquete grandules congelado
Un manojo perejil o cilantro, cortado

Lavar y secar los pedazos de pollo quitando la grasa. En un sartén sobre fuego mediano, cocinar el pollo en aceite de oliva. Cuando esté cocido, sacar del sartén. Añadir ajo, cebolla, apio, zanahoria y aji rojo. Cocinar por 3 a 4 minutos. Añadir el arroz y mezclar hasta que el arroz esté transparente y aromático. Poner el pollo de nuevo en el sartén y agregar vino o vermut, mezclar bien. Añadir tomates, alcaparras, aceitunas, especias, caldo de pollo y agua. Poner a hervir y cocinar hasta que esté el arroz, añadir más caldo si es necesario. El plato debe de ser asopado. Cuando casi esté el arroz, añadir los grandules. Antes de servir, mezclar el cilantro o perejíl.

SIRVE 6

ENCHILADO LANGOSTINO (LOBSTER ENCHILADO)

Daisy Fuentes

½ cup olive oil

¾ cup onion, chopped

4 cloves garlic, chopped

½ cup red or green bell peppers, chopped

1 cup tomatoes, peeled, seeded and chopped

3 teaspoons parsley, chopped

1 can (6 ounces) tomato sauce

1 can (6 ounces) tomato puree

1 can (2 ounces) red peppers, chopped

1 bay leaf

1 teaspoon paprika (preferably Spanish paprika)

1 teaspoon salt and pepper (or to taste)

1 tablespoon dry cooking wine

1 lobster tail (cut in rings), 1½ to 2 pounds

In a large frying pan, warm oil. Mix in the onion, garlic, and bell peppers until tender. Add the tomatoes, parsley, tomato sauce, tomato puree, red peppers, bay leaf, paprika, salt, pepper, and dry cooking wine.

Cook on low heat for 20 minutes. Raise to medium heat and add lobster rings, then cook until they become an orange color (approximately 10 to 15 minutes). Serve with or over white rice (or with pasta).

You can add shrimp with the lobster or replace the lobster with shrimp. (Shrimp also cooks in 10 to 15 minutes.)

SERVES 4

½ taza aceite de oliva

¾ taza cebolla, cortada

4 dientes de ajo, cortado

½ taza ajíes rojos o verdes, cortados

1 taza tomates cortados, sin piel ni semillas

3 cucharitas perejil, cortado

1 lata (150 gramos) salsa de tomate

1 lata (150 gramos) puree de tomate

1 lata (50 gramos) pimientos rojos, cortados

1 hoja de laurel

1 cucharita pimentón

1 cucharita sal y pimienta (o al gusto)

1 cucharada vino seco para cocinar

1 rabo de langosta (cortada), 1 kilogramo

En un sartén grande, ponga a calentar el aceite. Mezclar la cebolla, ajo y ajíes hasta que se ablanden. Añadir los tomates, perejíl, pimientos rojos de lata, salsa de tomate y puré de tomate, hoja de laurel, pimentón, sal y pimienta, y vino seco.

Cocinar a fuego lento por 20 minutos. Subir el fuego a medio y añadir la langosta, cocinar por 10 a 15 minutos. Sirva con arroz blanco o con pasta.

En lugar de la langosta puede usar camarones, o ambos. (Los camarones se cocinan también en 10 a 15 minutos).

SIRVE 4

ONE OF MY FAVORITE THINGS TO DO IS GETTING TOGETHER FOR A HOME-COOKED DINNER WITH MY PARENTS, MY GRANDPARENTS, AND MY SISTER. WE ALL TAKE TURNS COOKING OUR FAVORITE DISHES. MY MOTHER IS FROM SPAIN AND MY FATHER IS CUBAN. I WAS BORN IN CUBA AND MY SISTER WAS BORN IN SPAIN. THIS TERRIFIC CULTURAL MIX IS EVIDENT IN THE FOODS WE MAKE. WE ALL SIT AROUND THE KITCHEN, SUPPORT THE ELECTED CHEF OF THE NIGHT, SHARE A BOTTLE OF RED WINE AND GREAT CONVERSATION (SOMETIMES EVEN A HEATED DISCUSSION). WHEN IT'S MY TURN, I USUALLY MAKE A SPANISH DISH CALLED LOBSTER ENCHILADO. IT'S ALWAYS A HUGE HIT, AND I HOPE YOU ENJOY AS MANY UNFORGETTABLE DINNERS WITH IT AS I HAVE.

Alex Garcia

BORN IN CUBA, ALEX GARCIA MOVED TO PUERTO RICO AT 15, BUT NOT WITHOUT MAKING A GREAT PERSONAL DISCOVERY. BEFORE HE MOVED, HE FOLLOWED IN THE FOOTSTEPS OF HIS BIG BROTHER, THEN EMPLOYED AS A WAITER. WHEN VACATION TIME BECKONED, ALEX WAS ASKED TO TAKE HIS BROTHER'S PLACE. THUS, HIS PASSION FOR RESTAURANTS WAS BORN, AND IT HAS NEVER LEFT.

AFTER TWO YEARS IN NORTHEAST-ERN UNIVERSITY'S HOTEL MANAGEMENT SCHOOL, HE MOVED ON TO THE CULI-NARY INSTITUTE OF AMERICA IN HYDE PARK. AFTER ADDING WHAT HE FELT TO BE THE NECESSARY SIDE OF THE "BEHIND THE SCENES" ORIENTATION OF BECOMING A RESTAURATEUR, HE WENT BACK TO COMPLETE HIS UNDERGRADU-ATE DEGREE IN HOSPITALITY AT FLORIDA INTERNATIONAL UNIVERSITY IN MIAMI.

HIS PROFESSIONAL TRAINING INTRO-DUCED HIM TO THE WORLD OF CLASSIC FRENCH CUISINE, AS HE WORKED UNDER ROBIN HAAS AT THE TURNBERRY ISLE RESORT. BUT ALEX NEVER FELT

EMPANADA DE QUESO (CHEESE EMPANADAS)

FOR THE FILLING:

1 medium white onion, diced
2 tablespoons butter
1 bunch spinach, cleaned, deribbed, and julienned

2 pounds Manchego cheese, grated
1 cup hazelnuts, ground coarsely
1 cup dark raisins

In a skillet, sauté onion in butter until translucent, then add the spinach. Cover skillet and let wilt (about 1 to 2 minutes). Cool and then combine with the cheese, hazelnuts, and raisins. Set aside.

FOR THE DOUGH:

3 cups all-purpose flour
2 tablespoons salt
¼ pound unsalted butter, chilled and cut into small cubes
1 egg, lightly beaten

3 tablespoons sherry vinegar or red wine vinegar
¼ cup plus 1 tablespoon ice water
2 eggs, beaten with 2 tablespoons water to make an egg wash

In a large mixing bowl, combine the flour and salt. With a pastry blender or two knives, cut in the chilled butter pieces until the mixture resembles coarse crumbs. Add the egg, vinegar, and water; mix until well blended. Turn the dough out onto a sheet of plastic wrap and knead gently until you have a smooth dough, only a few seconds. Wrap well and chill for at least 5 minutes.

On a lightly floured surface, roll half the chilled dough to ⅛ inch thick. (Keep the other half refrigerated until ready to use.) Cut out 4-inch squares. Spoon about 1 tablespoon of the filling slightly off center of each square. Moisten the edges of the dough with the egg wash and fold one corner over to the opposite corner to form a triangle. Seal the edges with the tines of a fork. Repeat with the remaining dough. Refrigerate the empanadas on greased or parchment-lined baking sheets for at least 30 minutes. Heat the oven to 375 degrees. Brush the tops of the empanadas with the remaining egg wash and bake until well browned, about 25 minutes.

EMPANADA DE QUESO

PARA EL RELLENO:

1 cebolla blanca mediana, picada

2 cucharadas mantequilla

1 manojo espinacas, lavadas y cortadas
   al estilo juliana

1 kilogramo queso Manchego, rallado

1 taza avellanas, molida en grueso

1 taza pasas negras

En un sartén, fría ligeramente la cebolla hasta que esté traslucida en la mantequilla, después agregue las espinacas. Cubra el sartén y deje cocer (de 1 a 2 minutos). Enfríe y después combine con el queso, avellanas y pasas. Guárdelas a un lado.

PARA LA MASA:

3 tazas harina

2 cucharadas sal

227 gramos mantequilla sin sal, fría y
   cortada en cubos

1 huevo, ligeramente batido

3 cucharadas vinagre de jerez ó vino tinto

¼ taza mas una cucharada de agua con
   hielo

2 huevos, batidos con 2 cucharadas de
   agua para hacer un lavado de huevo

En una olla de mezclar, combine la harina y la sal. Con la batidora o con dos cuchillos, cortar la mantequilla congelada en piezas hasta que la mezcla tenga una aparencia de boronas grandes. Agregue el huevo, vinagre y agua, mezcle hasta que esté bien batido. Voltee la masa en una hoja de plástico para cocinar y amase suavemente hasta que obtenga una masa suave, únicamente por unos segundos. Envuelva bien y congele durante por lo menos 5 minutos.

En una superficie ligeramente cubierta de harina, extienda la mitad de la masa a un grosor de ³⁄₁₀ de centímetro. (Mantenga la otra mitad refrigerada, hasta que esté lista para usarse.) Corte cuadros de 10 centímetros. Cucharee como una cucharada de relleno en el cuadro y un poquito fuera de centro. Humedezca las esquinas de la harina con el lavado de huevo y doble una esquina sobre la esquina opuesta formando un triángulo. Selle las orillas con los dientes de un tenedor. Repíta éste paso con el resto de la masa. Refrigere las empanadas sobre hojas engrasadas de hornear por lo menos 30 minutos. Caliente el horno a 375 grados F. Pase la superficie de las empanadas con el restante del huevo y cocine hasta que esté dorado, como unos 25 minutos.

Alex Garcia

COMPLETELY COMFORTABLE WITH SUCH CUISINE. IT WAS WHILE WORKING ALONGSIDE DOUGLAS RODRIGUEZ AT YUCA IN MIAMI THAT ANOTHER WORLD BEGAN TO APPEAR...THE OPPORTUNITY FOR ALEX NOT ONLY TO BRING HIS NATIVE CUISINE TO A SOPHISTICATED CLIENTELE BUT TO DO SO WITH HIGH STANDARDS. CLEARLY, THE STANDARDS SET BY YUCA LED ALEX TO REMAIN SOUS CHEF TO RODRIGUEZ, FAST BECOMING A "CELEBRITY" CHEF, AND MOVE WITH HIM TO OPEN PATRIA IN MANHATTAN IN 1994.

"I LOVE MY FOOD! CUBAN CUISINE HAS ALWAYS BEEN FORCED TO BE CREATIVE. THERE NEVER IS REGULARITY TO WHAT IS AVAILABLE IN THE MARKETPLACE. A HOUSEWIFE STILL HAS TO SHOP ALL DAY, COOKING FROM WHATEVER IS IN THE STORES. MY MOTHER WOULD MAKE A CHICKEN SOUP, THEN USE PARTS FOR A FRICASSEE, THEN USE THE WINGS FOR ANOTHER MEAL. THERE IS ALWAYS 100 PERCENT UTILIZATION, AND NO WASTE. SO PLANNING AHEAD IS A WAY OF LIFE. AND CUBAN CUISINE IS DELIGHTFUL—THE LEGUMES, THE RICE, THE STEWS, RICH FISH. AN ISLAND SURROUNDED BY WATER, ITS CUISINE WAS ALSO ALWAYS INFLUENCED BY SPAIN, ANOTHER COUNTRY SURROUNDED BY WATER. SO VERY FRESH, TROPICAL FISH IS SOMETHING I ALWAYS LOVED, AND IT BECAME FUN EATING."

IT WAS WHILE WORKING WITH DOUGLAS RODRIGUEZ, WITH WHOM A GREAT

Alex Garcia

BOND IS SHARED, THAT THE 26-YEAR-OLD ALEX DEVELOPED THE CONFIDENCE TO BRING HIS NATIVE "PEASANT" CUISINE TO AN ENTIRELY DIFFERENT CULTURE, WITH HIS STANDARDS OF SOPHISTICATION. YET, WHEN ALEX SPOKE OF HIS LAST VENTURE, HIS RESTAURANT ERIZO, ONE NOT ONLY HEARD OF EXPERIENCE RELEGATED TO THE DYNAMICS OF FINE COOKING BUT WITNESSED A UNIQUE EXECUTIVE CHEF AND ENTREPRENEUR IN THE MAKING...ONE WHO BEFORE THE DOOR OPENED, WAS WELL AWARE THAT IT WAS A TRUE BUSINESS THAT MUST BE FINELY TUNED, AND NOT JUST HIS MOTHER'S KITCHEN.

GRILLED SHRIMP WITH RUM GLAZE AND AVOCADO SALAD

FOR THE SHRIMP:

12 jumbo shrimp
2 cloves garlic, crushed

Olive oil
Salt and pepper to taste

Season the shrimp with garlic, olive oil, salt, and pepper and grill until done.

FOR THE RUM GLAZE:

2 cups rum
½ cup molasses
Rind of ½ lemon

1 cinnamon stick
2 pieces star anise
4 peppercorns

In a saucepan over medium heat, combine all ingredients and reduce until it becomes a glaze. Remove cinnamon, anise, and peppercorns before serving.

NOTE: This glaze can be used over most grilled or pan-seared fish.

FOR THE AVOCADO SALAD:

2 avocados, diced
1 tomato, diced
½ small red onion, diced

Juice of 2 limes
1 ounce olive oil
Salt and pepper to taste

Combine all ingredients in a bowl. Serve the avocado salad in a martini glass with three shrimps on top. Drizzle with the rum glaze.

SERVES 4

CAMARONES ASADOS CON GLASEADO DE RON Y ENSALADA DE AGUACATE

PARA EL CAMARÓN:

12 camarones gigante

2 dientes de ajo, machacado

Aceite de oliva

Sal y pimienta al gusto

Condimentar el camarón con ajo, aceite de oliva, sal y pimienta y ase hasta que esté cocido.

PARA EL GLASEADO:

2 tazas ron

½ taza melaza

Cáscara de ½ limón

1 palo canela

2 piezas de anís

4 granos de pimienta

En un sartén sobre fuego medio, combine todos los ingredientes y reduzca, hasta que se vea glazeado. Remover la canela, anís y granos de pimienta antes de servír.

NOTA: Este glaseado es usado en la mayoría de pescados asados y al sartén.

ENSALADA DE AGUACATE:

2 aguacates, picados

1 tomate, picado

½ cebolla roja pequeña, picada

Jugo de 2 limas

28 gramos aceite de oliva

Sal y pimienta al gusto

Combine todos los ingredientes en una olla, sazone con sal y pimienta. Sirva la ensalada de aguacate en un vaso de martini con tres camarones en la orilla de la copa. Rocíe con el glaseado de ron.

SIRVE 4

PINEAPPLE FRITTERS WITH RUM CARAMEL SAUCE

FOR THE PINEAPPLE FRITTERS:

1½ cups flour
1½ teaspoons baking powder
3 teaspoons sugar
½ teaspoon salt
1 egg
¼ cup milk
1 (20-ounce) can of pineapple chunks
  in their own juice
Cooking oil

Combine the first seven ingredients, putting the pineapple chunks in last. Use the juice from the can of pineapple chunks to adjust the consistency of the fritters so that they are moist, yet not too sticky. Fill a deep-sided saucepan about three-quarters full of oil and heat. Drop the fritters by teaspoon into hot oil and fry until golden brown.

FOR THE RUM CARAMEL SAUCE:

1 pound sugar
1 quart heavy cream
4 ounces anejo rum
2 teaspoons vanilla extract

Melt the sugar in a heavy-bottomed saucepan. Be careful to stir sugar constantly, over medium heat, with a wooden spoon until all lumps have been melted. Continue stirring until the sugar (caramel) is a deep reddish brown. In a separate bowl, combine the cream and rum. Stand back from the saucepan and add half of the cream/rum mixture to the sugar. The cream will boil vigorously and dissolve the caramel. When the boiling slows down, add the rest of the cream/rum mixture. Whisk until the caramel is thoroughly dissolved. Add the vanilla.

NOTE: This sauce is great for all desserts. Don't limit yourself to these fritters alone. Be creative and pour it over ice cream and cakes, too.

FRITAS DE PLATANO CON JARABE DE RON

Alex Garcia

PARA LAS FRITAS DE PIÑA:

1½ tazas harina

1½ cucharita polvo de hornear

3 cucharadas azúcar

½ cucharadita sal

1 huevo

¼ taza leche

1 lata pedazos de piña (560 gramos)
   en su jugo

Aceite de cocinar

Combine los primeros siete ingredientes agregando los pedazos de piña hasta el final. Use el jugo de la lata de piña para ajustar la consistencia de las fritas, para que se mantengan húmedas, pero no pegajosas. Llene un sartén profundo, como ¾ lleno de aceite y caliente. Agregue de cucharada en cucharada hasta que estén dorados.

PARA EL CARAMELO:

454 gramos azúcar

960 mililitros crema condensada

112 gramos ron añejo

2 cucharitas extracto de vainilla

Derrita en un sartén grueso el azúcar. Tenga cuidado de mezclar el azúcar a fuego medio con cuchara de madera hasta que se haya derritido. Continue hasta que el caramelo sea de un color marrón rojizo. En un recipiente separado combine la crema y el ron. Agregue la mitad de la mezcla de crema y ron al azúcar. La crema tendrá a hervír vigorozamente y disolverá el caramelo. Cuando la ebullición se menor, agregue el resto de la crema/ron. Mezcle hasta que el caramelo esté totalmente disuelto. Agregue la vainilla.

NOTA: Este jarabe es maravilloso para todos los postres. No se limite a solo estas fritas. Sea creativo y úsela sobre nieve y pasteles también.

Andy Garcia

HAVING LEFT MY NATIVE CUBA AT THE AGE OF FIVE, TO ME THESE RECIPES REPRESENT MY CULTURE, FAMILY, AND FRIENDS...ALL THE THINGS THAT I TREASURE IN LIFE.

MOJO CRIOLLO (CUBAN MARINADE)

2 heads garlic, peeled
Salt to taste
1 cup lime juice
2 cups corn oil

Fill a blender three-quarters full with peeled garlic. Add salt and cover with lime juice. Puree until it forms a fine paste. Warm the corn oil in a saucepan over medium heat. Whisk in the garlic puree. Turn off heat and let sit for several hours for flavors to blend.

Pour over meat, fish, or poultry as a marinade and let stand overnight. Use to marinate, baste, grill, or sauté. It is especially good on pork or poultry. Sliced or diced raw onions can be added to enhance marinade. Also, it can serve as a dipping sauce for fried green bananas or broiled or sautéed vegetables.

2 cabezas de ajo, peladas
Sal (a gusto)
1 taza jugo de limón verde
2 tazas aceite de maíz

Llenar la batidora a ¾ de su capacidad con el ajo. Añadir la sal al gusto y cubrir con el jugo de limón verde. Mezclar hasta que se forme una pasta. Calentar 2 tazas de aceite de maíz en un sartén sobre fuego medio. Mezclar rápidamente con el puree de ajo. Remover del fuego y dejar por varias horas para mezclar los sabores distintos.

Servir con carne, pescado, pollo como marinada y deje reposar durante la noche. Puede usarla para marinar, asar o saltear. Es especialmente buena sobre la carne de cerdo o el pollo. Cebollas en hodajas o picadas pueden ser agregadas para hacerlo mejor. También se puede usar como salsa con plátanos verdes fritos o vegetales asados o salteados.

PIERNAS (CUBAN PORK LEG)

1 20-pound pork leg, bone in with skin and fat (untrimmed)
¼ cup ground cumin
Salt

Rub pork leg with cumin and salt generously. Preheat oven to 450 degrees. Place pork skin down in roasting pan and sear 45 minutes. Lower to 350 degrees and cover tightly. Cook 4 hours, then uncover, turn leg over, and cook 2 more hours. When done, remove from oven and let sit 20 minutes before carving.

To make pork sandwiches, use crusty Cuban or Italian bread and top leftover pieces of pork with Mojo Criollo.

SERVES 30 TO 40

---

1 (9 kilogramos) pierna de cerdo con hueso
¼ vaso cumino
Sal

Frotar la pierna con el comino y sal al gusto. Poner en el horno a 450 grados con la piel de la pierna para abajo por 45 minutos. Bajar la temperatura a 350 grados y tapar bien. Cocinar por 4 horas, destapar, voltear la pierna y cocinar por dos horas más. Cuando esté hecha, remover del horno y dejar por 20 minutos antes de cortar.

Para hacer sandwiches, use pan Italiano o Cubano de corteza gruesa y ponga encima trozos de cerdo.

SIRVE 30 A 40

David Garrido

THERE ARE COOKS, THERE ARE CHEFS, AND THERE ARE ARTISTS. THEN THERE'S DAVID GARRIDO—A MASTER OF ALL THREE. AS EXECUTIVE CHEF OF JEFFREY'S, DAVID IS RESPONSIBLE FOR CREATING AND EXECUTING MENUS TO SATISFY AUSTINITES' SOPHISTICATED TASTES FOR FINE FOOD.

A CONSUMMATE FOOD AFICIONADO, CHEF DAVID'S KNOWLEDGE OF INGREDIENTS AND CUISINE SPANS THREE CONTINENTS. THE SON OF A MEXICAN DIPLOMAT, DAVID WAS BORN IN CANADA, GREW UP IN MEXICO, PUERTO RICO, AND COSTA RICA, AND WAS SCHOOLED IN SWITZERLAND. HE HAS SPENT THE PAST DECADE IN TEXAS, WORKING WITH SUCH ACCLAIMED CHEFS AS STEPHAN PYLES—FIRST AT BABY ROUTH'S AND ROUTH STREET CAFÉ, THEN HELPING HIM TO OPEN HIS STAR CANYON RESTAURANT LAST SUMMER—AND WITH BRUCE AUDEN, BOTH AT THE FAIRMOUNT HOTEL AND RESTAURANT BIGA IN SAN ANTONIO.

IN 1992, CHEF DAVID TOOK OVER THE REINS OF JEFFREY'S KITCHEN, WHERE

WILD MUSHROOMS WITH GUAJILLO RED PEPPER SAUCE

FOR THE WILD MUSHROOMS:

1 pound wild mushrooms (Portabello, shiitake, chanterelle, crimini)
2 cloves garlic, chopped
2 shallots, sliced in half
2 sprigs basil
2 sprigs thyme
1 sprig rosemary
2 tablespoons extra virgin olive oil
Juice of ½ lemon
½ cup white wine
½ teaspoon sea salt

Preheat oven to 375 degrees. Rinse mushrooms lightly in cold water. In a stainless-steel pan, mix the garlic, shallots, basil, thyme, and rosemary. Place mushrooms on top of herbs. In a bowl, combine the olive oil, lemon juice, and wine, then sprinkle on top of mushrooms and season with salt. Cover with foil and cook for 30 minutes. Strain liquid and reserve.

FOR THE RED PEPPER GUAJILLO SAUCE:

1 teaspoon olive oil
2 shallots, chopped
2 red peppers, cut into small pieces
1 guajillo chili
1½ teaspoons fresh marjoram, chopped
¾ cup white wine
1 teaspoon sea salt
1½ teaspoons sugar
1 cup couscous

In a medium-sized pan, add the olive oil and sauté the shallots, red peppers, guajillo chili, and marjoram for 1 to 2 minutes; add wine, salt, and sugar; and bring to a boil. Cook for 2 minutes and transfer to a blender. Puree until smooth and strain. Set aside.

In a stainless-steel bowl, pour 2 cups of the hot mushroom liquid into the couscous and cover for 4 minutes. Uncover and separate grains softly with a fork, season with sea salt, and divide onto four plates. Divide mushrooms and place them next to the couscous. Spoon sauce around and serve.

SERVES 4

CHAMPIÑONES SALVAJES CON SALSA DE CHILES GUAJILLOS

David Garrido

POR LOS HONGOS SALVAJES:

454 gramos champiñones salvajes
    (Portabello, shiitake, chanterelle, crimini)
2 dientes de ajos, cortados
2 cebollitas, rebanadas por la mitad
2 ramas de albahaca
2 ramas de tomillo

1 rama de romero
2 cucharadas aceite de oliva extra virgen
Jugo de ½ limón
½ taza vino blanco
½ cucharita sal de mar

Precaliente de horno a 375 grados F. Enjuague las champiñones ligeramente en agua fría. En una cacerola limpia hecha de acero, mezcle el ajo, las cebollitas, tomillo, y romero. Poner los champiñones encima de las hierbas. En un cuenco combine el aceite, jugo de limón y vino. Rocíe encima de las champiñones y sazone con sal. Tape con papel de aluminio y cocine por 30 minutos. Cuele el líquido y reserve para el cuscús.

PARA LA SALSA DE CHILES GUAJILLOS:

1 cucharita aceite de oliva
2 cebollitas cortadas
2 pimientos rojos cortados en pedazos
    pequeños
1 chile guajillo
1½ cucharitas mejorana fresca, picada

¾ taza vino blanco
1 cucharita sal de mar
1½ cucharitas azúcar
1 taza cuscús

En una cacerola de tamaño mediano agregue aceite de oliva y saltée las cebollitas, pimientos rojos, guajillo y mejorana por 1 a 2 minutos, agregue vino, sal y azúcar y obtenga un hervor. Cocínelo por 2 minutos y transfiera a una batidora, puré hasta que esté liso y cuele. Déjelo a un lado.

En un cuenco del acero ponga dos tazas de líquido caliente de las champiñones en el cuscús y tape por cuatro minutos. Destape y separe granos suavemente con un tenedor, sazone con la sal y divida en cuatro platos. Divida las champiñones y póngalos al lado del cuscús. Ponga la salsa alrededor y sirva.

SIRVE 4

HE HAS ADDED HIS OWN TWIST TO THE NEW TEXAS CUISINE PIONEERED BY PYLES. WORKING WITH A NETWORK OF LOCAL FARMERS AND WHOLESALE PRODUCE VENDORS, DAVID USES THE FRESHEST INGREDIENTS AVAILABLE TO HIM, NEVER RELYING ON CANNED OR PROCESSED FOODS. HE INSTINCTIVELY KNOWS THE INTRICATE FLAVORS OF FOODS, BLENDING VARIOUS HERBS, SPICES, CHILIES, AND FRESH VEGETABLES INTO FRESH SALSAS, SAUCES, AND SIDE DISHES TO BRING OUT THE MOST SUBTLE QUALITIES OF MEAT, FISH, OR PASTA ENTREES.

IN A RECENT ISSUE OF BON APPETIT MAGAZINE, FOOD AND WINE CRITIC ALAN RICHMAN WROTE, "YOUNG CHEF DAVID GARRIDO...COULD BECOME THE FIRST CHEF EVER CELEBRATED IN A COUNTRY-AND-WESTERN SONG."

THE ACCOLADES KEEP ROLLING IN: IN NOVEMBER 1995, DAVID WAS INVITED TO COOK AT THE ESTEEMED JAMES BEARD HOUSE IN NEW YORK, AFTER WINNING TWO AWARDS AT THE TEXAS HILL COUNTRY WINE AND FOOD FESTIVAL IN SEPTEMBER OF 1997, DAVID JOINED THE FINEST CHEFS IN THE COUNTRY AT STAR CANYON IN DALLAS FOR AN EVENT HOSTED BY BON APPETIT MAGAZINE TO BENEFIT THE MAKE-A-WISH FOUNDATION.

David Garrido

DUCKLING NACHOS WITH HABANERO AIOLI, CHIPOTLE, AND MANGO PICO

FOR THE MARINADE:

3 chipotle chilies

¾ cup hot water

3 (6-ounce) boneless, skinless duckling breasts, thinly sliced

Puree chipotle chilies with hot water in a food processor. Marinate the duckling in this sauce for 10 minutes before cooking.

FOR THE YUCCA ROOT CHIPS:

1½ yucca roots, peeled, thinly sliced

Hot water, as needed

Oil, as needed

Sea salt, as needed

Soak the yucca in hot water for 15 minutes; dry. Deep fry in oil at 375 degrees for 1 to 1½ minutes or until light brown. Season with salt.

FOR THE HABANERO AIOLI:

3 tablespoons mustard

¼ cup honey

¾ cup cilantro, chopped

1½ tablespoons Habanero chilies, seeded and chopped

3 egg yolks

1½ tablespoons lemon juice

¾ teaspoon sea salt

¾ cup olive oil

Puree all ingredients except the oil. While pureeing, slowly add oil; refrigerate.

FOR THE MANGO PICO:

¾ cup mango, diced

¾ cup tomatoes, diced

½ cup onion, diced

½ cup cilantro, chopped

1½ tablespoons lemon juice

¼ teaspoon sea salt

Combine all ingredients in a bowl.

FOR THE PREPARATION:

Oil

Nacho chips

Heat a sauté pan over medium heat until hot. Put the duck skin side down and cook until skin is crisp, 2 to 3 minutes. Turn breasts and cook about 5 minutes for medium-rare, 7 minutes for medium. Place yucca chips on plate. Top with duck, Habanero aioli, and mango pico. Serve immediately.

SERVES 6

NACHOS DE PATO CON AIOLI HABANERO, CHIPOTLE Y MANGO PICO

PARA EL ADOBADO:

3 chiles chipotle

¾ taza agua caliente

3 (170 gramos) pechugas de pato sin piel ni huesos, finamente rebanadas

Haga los chiles chipotle puré con agua. Marine el pato en salsa por 10 minutos antes de cocinar.

PARA LAS REBANADAS DE YUCA:

1½ yucas, peladas y rebanadas finamente

Aqua caliente, según se requiera

Aceite, según se requiera

Sal de mar, según se requiera

Remoje las rebanadas de yuca en agua por 15 minutos; seque. Fría en aceite a 375 grados F por 1 a 1½ minutos o hasta que esté dorada. Sazone con sal.

PARA EL AIOLI HABANERO:

3 cucharadas mostaza

¼ taza miel

¾ taza cilantro, cortado

1½ cucharadas chilies Habanero sin semillas, cortados

3 yemas de huevo

1½ cucharadas jugo de limón

¾ cucharita sal de mar

¾ taza aceite de oliva

Haga puré todos los ingredientes, excepto aceite. Mientras esté haciendo el puré, despacio agregue aceite; refrigere.

PARA EL MANGO PICO:

¾ taza mango, picado

¾ taza tomates, picado

½ taza cebolla, picado

½ taza cilantro, picado

1½ cucharadas jugo de limón verde

¼ cucharita sal de mar

Combina todos los ingredientes para pico del mango.

PARA PREPARACIÓN:

Aceite

Nachos

Caliente el sartén a fuego medio hasta que esté caliente. Ponga el pato con la piel hacia abajo y cocine hasta que la piel esté crujiente, 2 a 3 minutos. Dé la vuelva a las pechugas y cocínelas por 5 minutos si las quiere poco a medio hechas, 7 minutos si las quiere al punto.

SIRVE 6

PEANUT-MINT CRUSTED TUNA WITH CILANTRO-LEMON SAUCE AND POMEGRANATE

FOR THE PEANUT-MINT CRUST:

½ cup peanuts

¼ cup flour

1 cup mint leaves

Prepare the Peanut-Mint Crust by combining all ingredients in a food processor, pulsing until well mixed. Set aside.

FOR THE CILANTRO-LEMON SAUCE:

1 tablespoon butter

4 cloves garlic, sliced

½ leek, white part only, rinsed and diced

2 serrano chilies, sliced

Juice of 1 lemon

¾ cup cream

½ cup plain yogurt

½ bunch cilantro, stems removed

Over medium heat in a medium sauté pan, cook butter, garlic, leek, and serranos for 3 to 4 minutes. Add lemon juice and simmer for 2 minutes. Add cream and yogurt and bring to a boil. Transfer to a blender, add cilantro, and puree until smooth. Strain and set aside in a warm spot.

FOR THE VEGETABLES:

1 tablespoon sesame seeds

1 teaspoon sesame oil

6 ounces snow peas, stems removed

12 cherry tomatoes

8 fresh basil leaves, chopped

1 tablespoon rice wine vinegar

¼ teaspoon sea salt

In a small sauté pan, toast sesame seeds until light brown. Add sesame oil, snow peas, tomatoes, and basil and cook for 2 minutes. Deglaze the pan with rice wine vinegar and season with salt. Serve immediately or reheat briefly before serving.

FOR THE TUNA STEAKS:

¼ cup plain yogurt

1 tablespoon water

4 (4-ounce) fresh tuna steaks

Salt to taste

4 tablespoons olive oil

½ cup pomegranate seeds (for garnish)

Cherry tomatoes (for garnish)

Mix yogurt with water in a small bowl. Season the tuna with salt, coat with the yogurt mixture and then the Peanut-Mint Crust, making sure the steaks are well coated. Heat the tablespoons olive oil in a large sauté pan over medium heat and cook the steaks for 2 minutes on each side per inch thickness. Divide the steaks among four plates, arranging the snow peas around them. Spoon the sauce over the steaks and garnish with pomegranate seeds and cherry tomatoes.

SERVES 4

ATÚN CON CORTEZA DE CACAHUETE Y MENTA, ADEREZADO CON SALSA DE CILANTRO-LIMÓN Y GRANADA

PARA LA CORTEZA DE CACAHUETE Y MENTA:

¼ taza de cacahuetes

¼ taza harina

1 taza de hojas de menta

Prepare la corteza de cacahuete y menta, combinando todos los ingredientes en el procesador de alimentos, pulsando hasta que esté todo bien incorporado. Póngalo a un lado.

PARA LA SALSA DE CILANTRO Y LIMÓN:

1 cucharada mantequilla

4 dientes de ajo, cortados

½ puerro, parte blanca sólo, lavado y cortado en cubitos

2 chiles serranos, rebanados

Jugo de un limón

¾ taza crema

½ taza yogurt

½ racimo cilantro, sin tallos

A fuego medio en una sartén mediana, cocine la mantequilla, ajo, puerro y chiles serranos por 3 a 4 minutos. Agregue el jugo de limón y deje hervir por 2 minutos. Añadir la crema y yogurt y deje hervir. Pase todo a la batidora, agregue el cilantro y hágalo puré. Cuele y guarde a un lado en un lugar templado.

PARA LOS VEGETALES:

1 cucharada ajonjolí

1 cucharadita aceite de ajonjolí

168 gramos guisantes en vaina plana

12 tomates tipo cereza

8 hojas de albahaca, picadas

1 cucharada vinagre de arroz

¼ cucharadita sal de mar

En un sartén pequeño, tueste el ajonjolí hasta que esté dorado. Agregue el aceite de ajonjoli, guisantes, tomates y albahaca y cocine por 2 minutos. Añadir el vinagre y sazone con sal. Sirva inmediatamente o recaliente un poco antes de servir.

PARA EL ATÚN:

¼ taza yogurt natural, sin sabor

1 cucharada agua

4 rodajas de atún fresco (112 gramos cada uno)

Sal al gusto

4 cucharadas aceite de oliva

½ taza semillas de granada (para decorar)

Tomates tipo cereza (para decorar)

Mezcle agua con yogurt en un recipiente pequeño. Sazone el atún con sal, cubra con la mezcla de yogurt y después con la mezcla de menta y cacahuete, asegurándose de que el atún esté bien cubierto. Caliente 4 cucharadas de aceite en un sartén grande a fuego medio y cocine el atún por 2 minutos (por cada 2½ centímetros de grosor) en cada lado. Divida el atún en cuatro platos, arreglando los guisantes alrededor. Ponga la salsa sobre el atún y decore con los tomates y granada.

SIRVE 4

Jackie Guerra

MY MOTHER INVENTED THIS RECIPE FOR ME WHEN I WAS IN COLLEGE. SHE WOULD MAKE IT FOR ME, AND I WOULD WARM IT UP AND PULL IT OUT OF THE OVEN AS IF I HAD COOKED IT. ALSO, THE LEFTOVERS COULD KEEP ME GOING FOR A WEEK.

CACEROLA DE TORTILLA DE POLLO (CHICKEN TORTILLA CASSEROLE)

3 chicken breasts
1 rib celery
1 onion, sliced
Salt and pepper to taste
1 container (8 ounces) sour cream
1½ cups chicken broth

1 can (14½ ounces) cream of chicken soup
1 can Ortega dried green chilies
1 small package corn tortillas (torn into small pieces)
1 cup Cheddar cheese, shredded

Place the chicken breasts in a saucepan with the celery, onion, salt, and pepper. Bring to a boil, skim off scum, then simmer for 15 to 20 minutes or until tender. Let cool, then shred the meat. Set aside.

Mix the sour cream, chicken broth, cream of chicken soup, and chilies. In an 11 x 13 casserole dish, layer the sour cream mixture, then the torn tortillas and chicken. Refrigerate for 24 hours. Top with the Cheddar cheese and bake at 325 degrees for 1 hour.

SERVES 4

---

3 pechugas de pollo
1 apio
1 cebolla rabanada
Sal y pimienta (al gusto)
1 paquete crema agria (225 gramos)
1½ tazas caldo de pollo

1 lata sopa de crema de pollo (400 gramos)
1 lata chiles cortados de Ortega
1 paquete tortillas, cortada en pedazos a mano
1 taza queso Cheddar, rallado

Poner pechugas en un sartén con apio, cebolla, sal y pimienta. Poner a hervir por 15 a 20 minutos. Dejar enfriar un poco y cortar el pollo. Poner a un lado.

Mezclar la crema agria, sopa de crema de pollo y chiles. En una cacerola de 28 x 33 centímetros, poner la mezcla de crema agria, poner las tortillas cortadas encima, y después el pollo. Poner en el refrigerador por 24 horas. Poner el queso encima y poner en el horno a 325 grados por una hora.

SIRVE 4

BUDIN DE PAN BUENO (BREAD PUDDING BUENO)

4 slices white bread (about 3 cups cubed)
4 eggs
1¾ cups milk
1 cup sugar
1 teaspoon vanilla

½ teaspoon salt
½ teaspoon cinnamon
¼ teaspoon nutmeg
1 cup Sun-Maid Baking Raisins
½ cup slivered almonds

FOR THE CARAMEL:
¼ cup water

½ cup sugar

Heat oven to 350 degrees. Grease a 8½ x 4½-inch glass loaf pan. Cut the bread slices into 1-inch cubes. Beat eggs in a large bowl. Stir in milk, sugar, vanilla, salt, cinnamon, and nutmeg. Add bread to mixture and set aside for 10 minutes. To prepare caramel, boil water and add sugar. Stir until sugar dissolves. Cook, stirring occasionally, just until mixture turns amber color; watch carefully. Pour into loaf pan and tilt pan to coat all sides. Stir the raisins and almonds into bread mixture. Pour mixture into loaf pan, place on a baking sheet, and bake in the center of the oven 60 to 70 minutes or until a knife inserted in the center comes out clean. Cool slightly and serve warm with whipped cream if desired.

SERVES 6 TO 8

---

4 rebana pan blanco (aproximadamente 3 tazas, en cubos)
4 huevos
1¾ tazas de leche
1 taza de azúcar
1 cucharita de vainilla

½ cucharita de sal
½ cucharita de canela
¼ cucharita de nuez moscada
1 taza pasas Sun-Maid para hornear
½ taza almendras en rajas

POR EL CARAMELO:
¼ taza de agua

½ taza de azúcar

Caliente el horno a 350 grados. Engrase la cacerola de vidrio para pan de 21½ x 11½ centímetros. Corte las rebanadas de pan en pedazos de 2½ centímetros. Los huevos se baten en un recipiente grande. Agregue la leche, azúcar, vainilla, sal, canela y nuez moscada. Agregue el pan a la mezcla y ponga a un lado por 10 minutos. Para preparar el caramelo, el agua se hierve y agregue azúcar. Revuelva el azúcar hasta que se disuelva. Cocine, revolviendo de vez en cuando, hasta que la mezcla se ponga de un color ambarino; vigile con cuidado. Eche en la cacerola de pan e incliné la cacerola para que todos los lados se cubran. Agregue las pasas para hornear y almendras en la mezcla del pan. Eche la mezcla en la cacerola de pan; ponga en una cacerola para hornear y hornée en el centro del horno por 60 a 70 minutos o hasta que un cuchillo insertado en el medio salga limpio. Deje que se enfríe un poco y sirva caliente con crema batida si desea.

SIRVE 6 A 8

Jose Hernandez [a.k.a. Chef Pepin]

SINCE CHEF PEPIN'S TELEVISION DEBUT IN 1988, HIS OUTGOING PERSONALITY AND CULINARY EXPERTISE HAVE BOOSTED RATINGS FOR *TV MUJER, HOLA AMERICA,* AND *AL MEDIODIA*—THREE OF THE MOST POPULAR SHOWS ON SPAN-ISH-SPEAKING TELEVISION. BILINGUAL, PEPIN HAS ALSO ATTRACTED ENGLISH-LANGUAGE AUDIENCES ON SHOWS LIKE LIFETIME CABLE NETWORK'S *ATTITUDES.*

CURRENTLY, PEPIN IS STARRING IN A TWO-HOUR TELEVISION SHOW, *DESPIERTA AMERICA,* FOR UNIVISION, WHICH AIRS ON 690 STATIONS IN AMERICA AND 26 COUNTRIES ABROAD. HE ALSO APPEARS IN *LA COCINA LATINA,* A SPANISH COOK-ING SHOW AIRING ON TELEMUNDO. PEPIN IS ALSO DEVELOPING A LATIN AMERICAN COOKING SHOW FOR THE UNITED FAMILY CHANNEL CALLED *LA COCINA DEL CHEF PEPIN.* HE RECENTLY RELEASED A LATIN COOKBOOK IN SPAN-ISH, *COOKING WITH CHEF PEPIN,* WITH

Jose Hernandez [a.k.a. Chef Pepin]

THE ENGLISH VERSION TO SOON FOL-LOW. PEPIN HAS BEEN FEATURED IN NUMEROUS HISPANIC NATIONAL TELEVI-SION COMMERCIALS AND NOTEWORTHY HISPANIC AND ENGLISH-LANGUAGE PRINT MEDIA: *MIAMI HERALD*, *READER'S DIGEST*, *CRISTINA*, *FLORIDA DESIGN* (FOR HIS KITCHEN), AND *MCI MAGAZINE*. PEPIN FREQUENTLY TAKES TIME OUT TO DONATE HIS TALENTS TO CHARITY WORK.

AS A CHILD IN CUBA, JOSE HERNAN-DEZ SPENT HOURS IN HIS GRAND-MOTHER'S KITCHEN, LEARNING HOW TO MAKE DELICIOUS PASTRIES FOR HIS FAMILY. DURING THOSE LESSONS, HE DEVELOPED A ZEST FOR LIFE AND COOKING THAT LED HIS GRANDMOTHER TO AFFECTIONATELY NICKNAME HIM "CHEF PEPIN." PEPIN SHARES HIS SPIRIT AND HUMOR WITH PEOPLE ALL OVER THE WORLD. AND, JUST AS HIS GRAND-MOTHER LOVED HAVING "CHEF PEPIN" IN HER KITCHEN, DAILY LETTERS FROM AROUND THE GLOBE INDICATE FANS FEEL THE SAME WAY.

IN 1960, PEPIN LEFT CUBA FOR FLORIDA, WHERE HE JUMPED ON THE FAST TRACK FOR HIS CULINARY CAREER. SINCE THEN, HE HAS REPRESENTED SUCH CLIENTS AS SUN-MAID BAKING RAISINS, GREEN GIANT, STOUFFERS, COCA-COLA, BORDEN, AND CRYSTAL SPRING WATER.

SALSA RÁPIDA SUN-MAID (SNAPPY SUN-MAID SALSA)

½ cup each diced red, yellow, and green bell peppers
1 cup Sun-Maid Baking Raisins
1 cup fresh pineapple, diced
½ cup red onion, diced
½ cup jicama, diced (optional)
¼ cup cilantro, finely chopped

½ jalapeño pepper, seeded and minced
3 tablespoons lime juice
1 small clove garlic, minced
½ teaspoon chili powder
¼ teaspoon ground cumin
¼ teaspoon salt

Combine all ingredients in a medium bowl. Cover and refrigerate for at least 1 hour for flavor to develop. Serve with chips as a dip, or as an addition to grilled fish or quesadillas.

MAKES 3 CUPS

½ taza cada uno pimientos rojos, amarillos y verdes cortados
1 taza pasas Sun-Maid para hornear
1 taza piña fresca cortada
½ taza cebolla roja cortada
½ taza jícama cortada (optativo)
¼ taza cilantro cortado finamente

½ chile jalapeño, desemillado y desmenuzado
3 cucharadas jugo de lima
1 diente de ajo pequeño, desmenuzado
½ cucharita de polvo de chile
¼ cucharita de comino remolido
¼ cucharita de sal

Combina todos los ingredientes en recipiente mediano. Cubra y refrigere por lo menos uno hora para desarrollar el sabor. Sirva con totopos, como una salsa, o como un adición a un pescado a la parrilla o quesadillas.

HACE 3 TAZAS

TORTILLA DE PATATAS ESPAÑOLA (SPANISH POTATO TORTILLA)

9 medium potatoes, finely chopped
Olive oil
1 onion, finely chopped lengthwise

Salt to taste
6 eggs

In a deep, nonstick skillet over low heat, place the potatoes and cover with enough olive oil to coat the potatoes, but not cover them. Add the onion and cook, stirring until browned. Add salt. Remove potatoes from the pan and set aside. In a separate bowl, crack open the eggs, then whisk with a fork until they just begin to froth. Drain the remaining oil from the pan, leaving just enough to barely cover the bottom. Turn heat to high. Add the beaten eggs to the potatoes and pour into skillet, shaking the pan to mix all the ingredients. Do not stir. Let the tortilla cook on one side until bottom has firmed and bubbles begin breaking through the surface of uncooked side. Once mixture has firmed, take a large plate and place over the pan. Working quickly, invert the tortilla onto the plate and place back in the pan to cook the other side. Remove from pan in the same manner.

SERVES 4

---

9 patatas (tamaño regular), cortada
Aceite de oliva
1 cebolla, cortada fina (a lo largo)

Sal al gusto
6 huevos

En un sartén hondo sobre fuego lento, poner las patatas con aceite suficiente para cubrir. Añadir la cebolla y freir hasta doradas. Añadir sal. Remover las patatas del sartén y poner en un colador para que pierdan el exceso de grasa. En un plato hondo, batir los huevos. Cuando estén bien batidos, agregar las patatas y la cebolla frita y agregarle sal al gusto. Nuevamente calentar el sartén, cuando esté caliente agregar una cucharita de aceite de oliva para cubrir el fondo del sartén. En este momento, agregar la mezcla de huevo, patata, y cebolla y dejar cuajar. Cuando esté media-durita, poner un plato llano mas grande que el sartén encima del sartén y voltear para que la tortilla esté en el plato. Volver a poner la tortilla en el sartén, esta vez del otro lado para que se termine de cocinar. Cuando esté la tortilla lista, servir en el mismo plato usado para voltearla cuando estaba cocida.

SIRVE 4

Enrique Iglesias

WHAT I LOVE ABOUT THE TORTILLA DE PATATAS ESPAÑOLA IS THAT YOU CAN HAVE IT FOR BREAKFAST, LUNCH, OR DINNER, OR EVEN AS LEFTOVERS. IT CAN BE EATEN HOT OR COLD, HOWEVER YOU PREFER, AND IT IS ALWAYS DELICIOUS!

WHEN I WAS IN SCHOOL AND WOULD FORGET TO BRING TORTILLAS DE PATATAS FOR LUNCH, I WOULD SEARCH TO SEE WHO HAD SOME SO I COULD EAT IT.

Julio Iglesias

TORTILLA "INDIAN CREEK"

Cooking oil
3 large (Idaho) potatoes, peeled and sliced
2 large onions, sliced
5 eggs, beaten
3 tablespoons water
Pinch salt

Fill a 12-inch skillet three-quarters full with oil and fry the potatoes and onions over medium heat until golden brown. Drain the fried onions and potatoes in a sieve, and put the oil into a separate container. To the beaten eggs, add the potatoes, onions, water, and salt to taste.

Heat 3 tablespoons of the reserved oil over medium-high heat and add the tortilla mix. Fry the mix until one side is almost cooked. Using a large plate, cover the skillet and flip the tortilla onto the plate and back into the skillet to cook the other side on medium-low heat.

SERVES 2

Aceite de cocinar
3 papas grandes (Idaho), pelada y cortada
2 cebollas grandes, cortadas
5 huevos, batidos
3 cucharadas agua
Sal al gusto

En un sartén de 30 centímetros, llenar ¾ con aceite y poner las cebollas y papas a calentar a fuego medio hasta que estén doradas. Colar el aceite y poner en otro recepiente. Añadir las papas y cebollas a los huevos batidos, 3 cucharadas de agua y sal al gusto.

Calentar 3 cucharadas del aceite reservado y sobre un fuego medio, calentar la mezcla. Calentar de un lado primero y luego con un plato más grande que el sartén, voltear la tortilla para cocinar el otro lado. Sobre un fuego lento.

SIRVE 2

DOÑA CHARO'S GAZPACHO ANDALUZ

2 large tomatoes, peeled
4 green bell peppers
2 red bell peppers
4 small cloves garlic
Salt to taste
Red wine vinegar to taste

Mix all ingredients in an electric blender or food processor, covered, at high speed until the vegetables are pureed. Pass mixture through a sieve and refrigerate.

FOR THE SIDE DISHES:
½ European cucumber, diced into tiny pieces
2 tomatoes, peeled and diced
1 onion, finely chopped
2 slices white bread, lightly toasted and diced

Refrigerate each ingredient separately in a small bowl and serve on the side with the Gazpacho Andaluz.

SERVES 2

---

2 tomates grandes, pelados
4 pimientos verdes
2 pimientos rojos
4 dientes de ajo
Sal al gusto
Vinagre de vino tinto al gusto

Mezclar todo los ingredientes en una batidora, tapar y hacer puré. Pasar la mezcla por un tamiz y poner en la nevera.

PARA LOS PLATOS ACOMPAÑANTES:
½ pepino Europeo, cortado finamente
2 tomates, pelados y cortados
1 cebolla, cortada finamente
2 trozos pan blanco, tostado y cortado.

Poner el la nevera en platos separados y servir con el Gazpacho Andaluz.

SIRVE 2

Julio Iglesias

John Leguizamo

WHEN I WAS GROWING UP IN JACKSON HEIGHTS, THE MELTINGEST POT OF THE BIG, ROTTEN APPLE, NEW YORK CITY. MONEY WAS TIGHT AND MY MOM WOULD DO WHATEVER SHE COULD IN THE KITCHEN WITH WHAT WE HAD. NOW MY MOM HAD NATURE AGAINST HER, 'CAUSE HER COOKING WAS SO BAD EVEN THE ROACHES WERE ORDERING OUT. BUT IT WASN'T HER FAULT. SHE HAD TO WORK 38 HOURS A DAY, 15 DAYS A WEEK (NO, I'M NOT BAD AT MATH, LATIN PEOPLE HAVE TO MAKE THE MOST OF THEIR TIME), SO SHE HAD NO TIME TO FINESSE HER CULINARY SKILLS. AND SHE'D SAY THINGS LIKE, "GOD PUT US ON EARTH TO SUFFER, NOW EAT UP" AND SHE'D SERVE US SOME MYSTERY DISH. I THINK SOME OF HER ALCHEMY CREATED NEW ELEMENTS.

SO WE REBELLED AND OPTED FOR SHAKE AND BAKE. WE ATE SHAKE AND BAKE EVERY DAY, RIGHT OUT OF THE BOX. AND WHEN THEY CAME UP WITH SHAKE

ARROZ CON POLLO (CHICKEN AND RICE)

1½ cups olive oil

10 cloves fresh garlic, finely chopped (divided use)

7 fresh scallions, finely chopped (divided use)

1 bunch cilantro

3½ teaspoons dried tarragon (divided use), crushed

Salt to taste

16 pieces chicken, 3 or 4 pieces for each person (use medium-sized pieces of chicken thighs or drumettes)

1 cup dry or semidry white wine

White and black pepper to taste (a few dashes of both are sufficient)

4 packets (17 ounces, 5 grams) Goya/Knorr Sazon seasoning with coriander and annatto (more if needed)

2 packets Goya powdered chicken bouillon (each is equal to one cube)

½ teaspoon ground cumin (less could be used according to taste)

1 package (8 ounces) frozen sweet peas, thawed

6 Spanish chorizos (The Goya brand is very good)

5 or 6 fresh red bell peppers, cut lengthwise into ½-inch slices

3½ cups rice

1½ Goya (9½ ounces, 269 mg) Manzanilla Spanish olives stuffed with minced pimientos (use less or more according to taste; drain before adding to rice)

In a 10-quart pot, heat ½ cup of oil over medium heat. Add 6 cloves of garlic and sauté for 2 minutes, then add 4 scallions, 3 or 4 twigs of cilantro, 2 teaspoons of tarragon, and a few dashes of salt. Sauté this mixture for another 2 minutes, then add the chicken and sauté for 4 minutes on each side. Add the wine, let simmer for 1 minute, then sprinkle with the black and white pepper, add 2 packets of Sazon, 1 packet of chicken bouillon, and ¼ teaspoon of cumin, and stir thoroughly. Add 11 cups of water and salt to taste.

Let simmer for 50 minutes, or less if you find that the chicken is tender before the prescribed time. Check constantly; the water should always be above the chicken. If you add more water, taste the broth for flavor and add more Sazon or salt if needed. The chicken should be firm when you finish cooking it. Take the chicken out of the pot, and put the broth in a separate pot/container.

While the chicken is cooking, in a separate pot cook the sweet peas for 1 minute, add ½ clove of garlic and a couple of dashes of salt. Leave the peas in this water until it is time to add them to the rice. Cut the chorizo into ¼-inch round slices and sauté them lightly in a frying pan in their own fat. Take the sautéed chorizo out of the pan and place on paper towels. Do not discard the fat. In the same pan that you sautéed the chorizo, add a little bit of oil and sauté the red peppers for 2 to 3 minutes. Save the chorizo, red peppers, olives, and capers to garnish the rice.

Add ¼ cup (or more if needed) of oil to the 10-quart pot and heat over medium heat. Add the rest of the garlic, scallions, 3 twigs cilantro, tarragon, a couple of dashes of both peppers, 2 Sazon packets, 1 chicken bouillon, and cumin. Let this mixture sauté for 2 minutes, then add the rice and sauté for 1 minute, stirring continuously.

Add the chicken and 9 cups of the broth that you reserved from the chicken. If you have less than 9 cups of broth, then add water, add salt to taste, and stir the entire mixture well. Let simmer over medium heat for 15 minutes, then reduce heat and remove the lid of the pot for about 5 to 10 minutes. Place the lid back on the pot.

AND BAKE BARBECUE IT WAS A NATIONAL FREAKIN' HOLIDAY. AND ON SPECIAL OCCASIONS SHE'D MAKE SUSHI: SHE'D OPEN UP A CAN OF TUNA AND SLAP IT ON RICE, AND WE PRETENDED WE LIVED IN SOHO. AND MY MOM CARED A LITTLE TOO MUCH FOR US. "AS PROOF OF MY LOVE, NENES, I'M GOING TO MAKE THE MILK FROM SCRATCH, NOT LIKE THOSE NEGLIGENT UPTOWN MOMS." AND SHE'D TAKE POWDERED MILK, HIDE IT IN HER PURSE, AND GO INTO THE HALL WITH A BUCKET. THEN WE'D HEAR THE PATHETIC MOO'S. SHE'D COME BACK WITH THIS LUMPY CONCOCTION. "FRESH DOESN'T TASTE AS GOOD AS STORE-BOUGHT." THEN MY MOM PUT HERSELF THROUGH COLLEGE, RAISED TWO BOYS BY HER LONESOME, AND IMPROVED HER COOKING SO MUCH THAT THIS DISH IS A TESTAMENT TO HER BRILLIANCE AND HER DRIVE AND A LATIN MOM'S LOVE AND DEVOTION.

THIS ARROZ CON POLLO MAKES ME HOLLER AND DANCE, IT TASTES SO DAMN GOOD. WHEN MY MOM MAKES IT, ME AND MY BROTHER GET GHETTO AND FIGHT FOR THE LEFTOVERS LA RASPA, "I'LL CUT YOU MOTHAF@#$!" IT TAKES HER DAYS AND HOURS AND THE TASTE IS FREAKIN' GLORIOUS. AMBROSIA TO THE GODS, HECATOMBS TO THE ANCIENT GREEKS.

WARNING: TRY NOT TO GET GHETTO WHEN YOU MAKE THIS DISH. I DARE YOU!

Check constantly. If you see that the rice is still not cooked, add more broth or water until the rice is tender. If water is added instead of broth, add some Sazon and salt to taste. Be careful not to add more broth/water than needed. When done, the Arroz Con Pollo should be tender and moist, but not juicy or watery.

Place the rice with the chicken in a large baking pan and add the drained sweet peas, chorizo, and olives, and mix everything gently. Then place the red peppers over the whole pan. Heat in the oven for 5 minutes before serving.

NOTE: Cook the chicken the day before you want to serve this recipe, and maintain it in its broth. Place chicken and broth together in the refrigerator until it is time to add it to the rice. The flavor of the chicken is highly enhanced.

SERVES 4 TO 6

ARROZ CON POLLO

1½ vasos aceite de oliva
10 dientes de ajo fresco, cortado finamente
7 cebollas verdes frescas, cortadas finamente
1 manojo cilantro
3½ cucharadas estragón seco aplastado
Sal (al gusto)
16 pedazos pollo, 3 a 4 pedazos por persona (muslos o contramuslos)
1 taza vino blanco, seco o semi-seco
Pimienta blanca y negra (al gusto)

4 paquetes Goya/Knorr Sazón con annatto y cilantro (más si es necesario)
2 paquetes Goya caldo de pollo en polvo (cubo de pollo en polvo)
½ cucharita comino (o al gusto)
1 paquete guisantes descongelados
6 chorizos Españoles
5 o 6 ajies rojos
3½ tazas arroz
1½ latas aceitunas Manzanilla Española con pimientos (al gusto, quite el líquido)

En una cazuela honda, ponga a calentar ½ taza de aceite sobre fuego medio. Añadir 6 dientes de ajo, cocer por dos minutos, agregar las cebollas verdes, 3 a 4 hojas de cilantro, 2 cucharitas de estragón, y un poco de sal. Mezclar esto por dos minutos más. Ahora agregar el pollo y cocinar por cuatro minutos en cada lado. Añadir el vino y hervir por un minuto. Agregar las pimientas blanca y negra, dos paquetes de Sazón, 1 paquete de caldo de pollo, ¼ cucharita de comino y mezclar bien. Añadir 11 vasos de agua y sal al gusto.

Dejar hervir por 50 minutos o menos si el pollo esta blando. Vigilar constantemente. El agua siempre debe estar arriba del pollo. Si agrega más agua, probar el caldo para el sabor y añadir más sazón o sal, si es necesario. El pollo debe de estar firme cuando esté cocido. Remover el pollo de la cazuela y poner el caldo en otro recipiente.

En lo que el pollo esté cocinándose, en otra cazuela, cocinar los guisantes por un minuto, añadir ½ diente de ajo, cortado fino y un poco de sal. Dejar los guisantes en esta agua hasta que sea tiempo de añadirlo al arroz. Cortar los chorizos y cocinarlo en un sartén en su propia grasa. Remover los chorizos y poner en una toalla de papel. En el mismo sartén que cocinaste los chorizos, agregar un poco de aceite y cocinar los ajíes rojos cortados por 2 a 3 minutos. Separar los chorizos, aceitunas, y ajíes para añadir al arroz.

Añadir ¼ taza de aceite a la cazuela honda sobre fuego medio. Agregar el resto del ajo, cebollas verdes, 3 hojas de cilantro, estragón, un poco de ambas pimientas, 2 paquetes de sazón, 1 caldo de pollo y comino. Dejar cocinar por 2 minutos, añadir el arroz y cocinar por un minuto, mezclar.

Añadir el pollo y 9 tazas de caldo que separó del pollo. Si tiene menos de nueve vasos, añadir agua, y sal a gusto a la mezcla. Hervir sobre fuego medio por 15 minutos, reducir el fuego y destapar y cocinar por 5 a 10 minutos más, tapar de nuevo. Cocinar hasta que el arroz esté blando.

Poner el arroz con el pollo en una cazuela pyrex. Añadir los guisantes, chorizos y aceitunas y mezclar todo. Sobre la mezcla ponga los ajíes rojos. Calentar en el horno por 5 minutos antes de servir.

NOTA: Cocinar el pollo el dia antes y mantener en su caldo. Poner el pollo y caldo en la nevera hasta que sea tiempo de añadir al arroz. Maximiza los sabores del pollo.

SIRVE 4 A 6

Jennifer Lopez

FLAN DE LECHE DE ABUELA JULIA

1 can (14½ ounces) Carnation condensed milk
5 eggs

1 cup sugar
1 teaspoon vanilla extract

FOR THE CARAMEL:
½ cup sugar

Heat the condensed milk, but not until boiling. Let cool slightly. Beat the eggs and sugar together until thoroughly combined. While milk is still warm, beat it into the egg-sugar mixture a little at a time, then add the vanilla.

Put the sugar in a pot over low heat. The sugar will start to liquefy and turn brown. Once it turns brown and is a syrupy consistency, remove from heat quickly. Don't let it burn! Pour into the flan pan (6- to 8-inch round pan). Pour it in quickly, as once you do, it hardens.

Pour the custard mixture over the caramel. Fill a separate baking pan halfway with water. Cover flan with aluminum foil and a rubber band. Put it into the pan with water and place it in the oven. Bake for 40 minutes at 350 degrees. Insert fork in middle and if the consistency is hard, it's done. Once it is done, place it in the refrigerator to cool. Serve cold.

SERVES 4

1 lata leche condensada Carnation (410 gramos)
5 huevos

1 taza azúcar
1 cucharita extracto de vainilla

PARA EL CARAMELO:
½ taza azúcar

Calentar la leche condensada, pero no hervir. Dejar enfriar un poco. Batir los huevos y azúcar juntos. En lo que la leche esté caliente, batir en la mezcla los huevos y azúcar, luego añadir la vainilla.

Tomár el azúcar y poner sobre fuego lento. El azúcar se convierte en líquido. ¡Cuando esto sucede, remover del fuego, sin dejar quemar! Poner en un molde de flan (redondo de 15 a 20 centímetros) rápidamente. Se endurecerá.

Poner la mezcla sobre el caramelo. Tomar otro recipiente y llenar la mitad con agua. Tomar el flan y cubrir con papel de aluminio y una liga. Poner en el recipiente con agua y poner en el horno por 45 minutos a 350 grados. Meter un tenedor por el centro, si está duro, está listo. Cuando esté listo, poner en la nevera hasta que se enfríe. Servir frio.

SIRVE 4

LOBSTER GAZPACHO

2 to 2½ pounds lobster, or 2 smaller
   lobsters

1 quart court bouillon (herb broth)

FOR THE BROTH:

1 can (46 ounces) tomato juice
¾ cup rice vinegar
2 tablespoons extra virgin olive oil
¾ cup sake
1½ teaspoons soy sauce
1 cup dry white wine

1 tablespoon plus 2 teaspoons ground
   fresh green coriander seeds (much less
   if you're using dried coriander)
Sea salt
Freshly ground white pepper

FOR THE VEGETABLES:

½ cup tender young green beans
½ cup sweet peas or sugar snap peas
2 Japanese cucumbers, peeled and
   sliced lengthwise, or 1 regular cucumber,
   peeled, seeded, and finely diced
1 cup red bell pepper, minced
1 tablespoon fresh lemon grass, finely
   minced

1 cup red tomatoes, seeded and diced
½ cup yellow tomatoes (or use all red if
   yellow are unavailable), seeded and
   diced
2 jalapeños, seeded and minced

FOR THE GARNISH:

1 tablespoon chives, minced
5 tablespoons scallion or red onion,
   minced

3 tablespoons cilantro, minced
2 tablespoons fresh basil, minced

Cook the lobster in boiling bouillon for 8 to 12 minutes, depending on the size. Cool, then remove the meat from the shell and cut into ½-inch chunks (you should have about ¾ pound of meat). Refrigerate.

Mix together all the broth ingredients and chill.

Cut the beans and sugar snap peas into 1-inch lengths. Blanch the beans and peas in lightly salted boiling water for 1 minute. Remove them and rinse in cold water. Combine with the remaining vegetables and mix into the broth.

Combine the chives, scallion or red onion, cilantro, and basil and set aside. To serve, divide the lobster equally into two bowls. Ladle the vegetable broth over the lobster, and sprinkle with some of the garnish.

SERVES 2

A Martinez

THIS IS A SOUP SO SUCCULENT AND DIVINE THAT YOU'D THINK YOU WERE DINING ON PRINCE EDWARD ISLAND, RATHER THAN IN THE COMFORT OF YOUR OWN KITCHEN. THIS IS A FAVORITE SUNDAY NIGHT SPECIALTY IN OUR HOME. AFTER A DAY OF RUNNING AROUND, IT'S NICE TO RELAX WITH MY WIFE AND KIDS WITH THIS SPECIAL FAMILY RECIPE.

GAZPACHO DE LANGOSTA

1 kilogramo langosta

.95 litro caldo (receta sigue)

PARA EL CALDO:

1 lata jugo de tomate

³/₄ taza vinagre de arroz

2 cucharadas aceite de oliva

³/₄ taza sake (vino seco Japonés)

1½ cucharitas salsa de soja

1 taza vino seco blanco

1 cuchara + 2 cucharitas semillas de cilantro

Sal de mar

Pimienta blanca molida

PARA LOS VEGETALES:

½ taza judías verdes

½ taza guisantes verdes

2 pepinos Japonés, pelados y cortados

1 taza ají rojo, cortado

1 cucharada hierba de limón, cortada

1 taza tomates rojos, cortados y sin semilla

½ taza tomates amarillos, cortados (o rojas si no hay amarillos)

2 chiles jalapeños, sin semillas y cortados

PARA PONER ENCIMA:

1 cucharada cebollana, cortada

5 cucharadas cebollitas verdes o cebollas rojas, cortadas

3 cucharadas cilantro, picado

2 cucharadas albahaca, picada

Cocinar la langosta en el caldo por 8 a 12 minutos, depende del tamaño. Dejar enfriar, y remover la carne de la cáscara y cortarla en trozos de 1¼ centímetros (más o menos 340 gramos carne). Poner en la nevera.

Mezclar todo los ingredientes para el caldo y poner a enfriar.

Cortar judías verdes y poner con los guisantes en agua hirviendo con sal por un minuto. Remover y lavar con agua fria. Mezclar con los ingredientes que quedan y poner en el caldo.

Mezclar los cebollanas, cebollitas verdes, cilantro, y albahaca y poner a un lado. Para servir, dividir la langosta en cazuelas. Poner el caldo encima y al finalmente los ingredientes de adorno.

SIRVE 2

A Martinez

Matt Martinez Jr.

MATT MARTINEZ JR. WAS BORN AND RAISED IN AUSTIN, TEXAS. HIS GRANDFATHER OPENED THE FIRST TEX-MEX RESTAURANT IN AUSTIN IN 1925. MATT GREW UP WORKING IN HIS FATHER'S AUSTIN RESTAURANT, MATT'S EL RANCHO.

AS A FOURTH-GENERATION TEX-MEX CHEF, MATT HAS CONTINUED HIS FAMILY'S TRADITION WITH THE DEVELOPMENT AND OPERATION OF MANY SUCCESSFUL RESTAURANT CONCEPTS, INCLUDING MATT'S RANCHO MARTINEZ (DALLAS, TEXAS), FEATURING HIS FAMOUS TEX-MEX FOOD. MATT'S NO PLACE (DALLAS, TEXAS) IS HIS CONCEPT IN TEXAS CUISINE. MATT IS THE FIRST CHEF TO REINTRODUCE UNIQUE "PRAIRIE/RANGE-STYLE" COOKING SINCE COWBOYS USED A SIMILAR TECHNIQUE. HIS OWN SPECIAL SEASONINGS, "TEXAS SPRINKLE" AND "BLACK MAGIC" FINISHING SAUCE, ENHANCE THE NATURAL FLAVOR OF ALL DISHES. HIS FOCUS IS ON INDIGENOUS HIGH-FLAVOR, LOW-FAT FOODS WITH SOUTHERN ROOTS.

JALAPEÑOS RELLENOS (STUFFED JALAPEÑOS)

(ADAPTED FROM *MATT MARTINEZ'S CULINARY FRONTIER*, DOUBLEDAY, 1997)

12 whole pickled jalapeños
2 cups grated Monterey Jack or American cheese
1 cup flour

2 cups buttermilk
2 cups cracker meal or seasoned bread crumbs
Oil of your choice for deep-frying

Slit open one side of each jalapeño and discard all the seeds and membranes. Rinse the jalapeños in cold water.

Stuff the jalapeños with the cheese, roll them in the flour, dunk them in buttermilk, then roll them in the cracker meal.

Place the stuffed jalapeños in the freezer for 2 to 3 hours until they are completely frozen.

Using enough oil to give you about an inch in depth, fry the peppers to a golden brown at 375 degrees. The entire batch should be ready in 3 to 4 minutes. The quicker you eat them after frying, the better they are.

SERVES 4 TO 6

(DEL LIBRO *MATT MARTINEZ'S CULINARY FRONTIER*, DOUBLEDAY, 1997)

12 jalapeños en vinagre, enteros
2 tazas queso Monterey Jack o Americano, rallado
1 taza harina

2 tazas suero de mantequilla
2 tazas pan rallado, sazonado
Aceite para freír

Abra una lado de cada jalapeño y saque las semillas y membranas. Lave los jalapeños en agua fría.

Rellene los jalapeños con el queso, páselos por harina, luego por el suero de mantequilla y después por el pan rallado.

Ponga los jalapeños rellenos en el congelados por 2 a 3 horas hasta que estén completamente congelados.

Usando suficiente aceite para dar 2½ centímetros de profundidad, fría los chiles a 375 grados hasta que estén dorados. Todos estarán listos en 3 a 4 minutos. Lo más rápido que se los coma después de freírlos, lo mejor que sabrán.

SIRVE 4 A 6

QUAIL

(ADAPTED FROM *MATT MARTINEZ'S CULINARY FRONTIER*, DOUBLEDAY, 1997)

3 slices bacon
8 quail, or 2 pounds other wild bird
3 tablespoons flour
½ cup finely chopped onion
½ cup finely chopped green bell pepper
¼ cup finely chopped celery
2 cups finely chopped fresh mushrooms
2 cups fresh or frozen corn kernels
1 teaspoon salt, plus extra, to taste
½ teaspoon black pepper, plus extra
   to taste

2 teaspoons crushed and finely chopped
   garlic
3 teaspoons ground cumin
1 tablespoon soy sauce
1 tablespoon brandy or whiskey
4 cups water
1 cup crushed tomatoes
Chopped green onion, as a garnish

In a skillet, sauté the bacon until crisp. Chop into small pieces. Leave 3 tablespoons of bacon drippings in the pan, and reserve the crumbled bacon bits.

Dust the quail in the flour, then sauté them in the bacon drippings for 4 to 5 minutes, or until the quail have browned.

Combine the onion, bell pepper, celery, mushrooms, corn, teaspoon of salt, ½ teaspoon black pepper, garlic, and cumin in the pan. Remove the quail.

Lightly sauté the vegetables for 2 to 3 minutes, until they are translucent. Add the soy sauce and brandy or whiskey, and sauté for 30 seconds to 1 minute. When it's all sautéed, add the water and crushed tomatoes.

Bring the sauce to a simmer, add the quail, and cover the pan (add more water, too, if dry; the sauce should be thick and pourable, but not lumpy). Simmer the quail for 30 minutes, or until they are tender.

Adjust the salt and pepper. Sprinkle the bacon bits on top, and garnish with chopped green onion.

NOTE: For maximum mouth-watering effect, serve the quail over steamed rice or buttered pasta.

SERVES 4

Matt Martinez Jr.

MATT HAS PERSONALLY DEVELOPED HUNDREDS OF RECIPES, SPICE COMBINATIONS, AND OPERATING PROCEDURES THAT ENSURE A UNIQUE, ENJOYABLE EXPERIENCE TIME AFTER TIME.

AT THE Y.O. RANCH RESTAURANT, HIS LATEST VENTURE, MATT HAS COLLABORATED WITH GENE STREET AND THE SCHREINER FAMILY FROM THE ORIGINAL Y.O. RANCH IN KERRVILLE TO CREATE SOME TEXAS LORE AT THE POPULAR DALLAS WEST END.

CODORNIZ

(DEL LIBRO *MATT MARTÌNEZ'S CULINARY FRONTIER*, DOUBLEDAY, 1997)

3 tiras de tocino

8 codornices, o 1 kilogramo de cualquier otro ave de caza

3 cucharadas harina

½ taza cebolla finamente picada

½ taza pimiento verde finamente picado

¼ taza apio finamente picado

2 tazas champiñones finamente picados

2 tazas granos de maíz, frescos o congelados

1 cucharadita sal, más extra al gusto

½ cucharadita pimienta negra, más extra al gusto

2 cucharaditas de ajo, finamente picado

3 cucharaditas de comino molido

1 cucharadita salsa de soja

1 cucharada aguardiente (brandy o whisky)

4 tazas agua

1 taza tomates machacados

Cebolla verde picada, para decorar

En un sartén, saltée el tocino hasta que esté crujiente. Córtelo en pedacitos. Deje 3 cucharadas de la grasa del tocino en el sartén y reserve los trocitos de tocino.

Pase las codornices por harina y salteelas en la grasa del tocino por 4 a 5 minutos o hasta que se hayan dorado.

Combine la cebolla, pimiento verde, apio, champiñones, maíz, cucharadita sal, ½ cucharadita pimienta, ajo y comino en el sartén. Saque las codornices.

Ligeramente saltée los vegetales por 2 a 3 minutos, hasta que estén transparentes. Agregue la salsa de soja y el aguardiente y saltée por 30 segundos a 1 minuto. Cuando todo esté salteado, agregue el agua y tomates.

Deje que la salsa hierva ligeramente, añada las codornices y cubra el sartén (agregue más agua también, si se reseca; la salsa deberá estar espesa, pero no llena de grumos). Déjelas hervir por 30 minutos o hasta que las codornices estén tiernas.

Ajuste la sal y pimienta. Espolvoree los trocitos de tocino encima, y decore con la cebolla verde.

NOTA: Para que se le haga agua la boca, sirva las codornices sobre arroz blanco o pasta en mantequillada.

SIRVE 4

Matt Martinez Jr.

FRIJOLES VEGETARIANOS BORRACHOS (VEGETARIAN DRUNK BEANS)

(ADAPTED FROM *MATT MARTINEZ'S CULINARY FRONTIER*, DOUBLEDAY, 1997**)**

1 pound (2 cups) pinto beans
6 cups water
1 cup coarsely chopped white onions
1 cup coarsely chopped celery
1 cup coarsely chopped green or red bell
   peppers
2 cloves garlic, crushed and finely
   chopped

½ small bay leaf
1 large whole zucchini
1 cup coarsely chopped fresh cilantro,
   loosely packed
½ bottle or can Lone Star beer
Salt and black pepper to taste

While drinking the half of the beer you won't be using in the recipe, put all the other ingredients into a large pot and bring to a boil. Just throw the whole zucchini into the pot. Cover and simmer on low heat for 2 hours. Then add the beer you haven't already swallowed.

Simmer on low heat for another 30 minutes to an hour, until the beans are tender. Season with salt and pepper.

NOTE: The zucchini adds a special sweetness to these beans. When serving, cut off a piece of zucchini for each bowl of beans.

SERVES 6 TO 8

(DEL LIBRO *MATT MARTÌNEZ'S CULINARY FRONTIER*, DOUBLEDAY, 1997**)**

454 gramos (2 tazas) frijoles pintos
6 tazas agua
1 taza cebolla picada
1 taza apio picado
1 taza pimiento verde o rojo picado
2 dientes de ajo, machacados finamente
   picados

½ hojas de laurel pequeño
1 calabacita grande
1 taza cilantro picado
½ botella o lata de cerveza "Lone Star"
Sal y pimienta al gusto

Mientras se beba la mitad de la cerveza que no usará en la receta, ponga todos los ingredientes en una olla grande y deje hervir. Ponga la calabacita entera en la olla. Cubía y déjelo hervir a fuego lento por 2 horas. Después agregue la cerveza que no se haya bebido.

Hierva a fuego lento por 30 minutos a 1 hora más, hasta que los frijoles estén blandos. Sazone con sal y pimienta

NOTA: La calabacita agrega un toque dulce a los frijoles cuando los sirva, ponga un trozo de calabacita en cada plato de frijoles.

SIRVE 6 A 8

ARROZ CON CREMA Y CHILES POBLANOS (CREAMY RICE CASSEROLE WITH POBLANO CHILIES)

(ADAPTED FROM *FOOD FROM MY HEART*, MACMILLAN, 1992)

4 cups water
1 tablespoon butter
2 teaspoons salt, or to taste
2 cups converted rice
2 tablespoons vegetable oil
1 small onion, chopped (about ½ cup)
1 clove garlic, minced
2 poblano chilies, roasted, peeled, seeded, deveined, and diced

2 cups fresh corn kernels or 1 package (10 ounces) frozen corn kernels, thawed, or 1 can (16 ounces) corn, drained
1½ cups Crema Agria Preparada (see recipe below)
½ pound white Cheddar cheese, shredded

Bring the water to a boil in a medium-size saucepan over high heat and add the butter and salt. When the butter has melted, add the rice and bring to a boil. Reduce the heat to very low, cover the saucepan tightly, and cook for 20 minutes. Remove the rice from the pan and spread on a baking sheet to cool, or allow to cool in the pan uncovered.

Meanwhile, preheat the oven to 350 degrees (if using a Pyrex baking dish, set the oven at 325 degrees).

Heat the oil in a heavy skillet over medium-high heat until very hot but not quite smoking. Reduce the heat to medium, add the chopped onion and garlic, and cook, stirring until wilted, 2 to 3 minutes. Add the poblanos and cook, stirring for 1 minute. Let cool, then combine with the rice. Mix in the corn, sour cream mixture, and shredded cheese.

Pour the mixture into a heatproof baking dish or casserole and bake until heated through, about 30 minutes.

SERVES 6

FOR THE CREMA AGRIA PREPARADA (AROMATIC SOUR CREAM MIXTURE):
2 cups cultured sour cream
1 small onion, finely chopped (about ½ cup)
1 small garlic clove, minced
2 tablespoons finely chopped cilantro leaves
Salt to taste

Combine all the ingredients and let rest 5 minutes to blend the flavors.

YIELDS 2 CUPS

Zarela Martinez

ZARELA MARTINEZ, ONE OF THIS GENERATION'S LEADING U.S. RESTAURATEURS, WAS BORN AND RAISED IN MEXICO BUT BEGAN COOKING PROFESSIONALLY DURING THE LATE 1970s IN EL PASO, TEXAS. WITH THE ENCOURAGEMENT OF PAUL PRUDHOMME AND CRAIG CLAIBORNE, WHO HAD BEEN IMPRESSED BY HER VIVID MEXICAN FOOD, SHE MADE SOME NATIONALLY NOTED GUEST-CHEF APPEARANCES AND IN 1983 MOVED HER BUSINESS TO NEW YORK. HERE, SHE QUICKLY MADE HER MARK AS MENU DESIGNER AND LATER EXECUTIVE CHEF FOR CAFÉ MARIMBA, THE CITY'S FIRST SERIOUS ATTEMPT AT RECREATING REGIONAL MEXICAN CUISINE WITH LOCAL RESOURCES. A LOYAL FOLLOWING OF DINERS AND FOOD WRITERS RESPONDED EAGERLY WHEN IN 1987 SHE DECIDED TO START HER OWN RESTAURANT, ZARELA.

SINCE ITS OPENING, ZARELA HAS BECOME BELOVED AS A STIMULATING MEETING PLACE IN NEW YORK AND A BENCHMARK OF CULINARY EXCELLENCE. IT REGULARLY WINS SUPERLATIVE

Zarela Martinez

ARROZ CON CREMA Y CHILES POBLANOS

(DEL LIBRO *FOOD FROM MY HEART*, MACMILLAN, 1992)

4 tazas agua
1 cucharada mantequilla
2 cucharaditas sal, o al gusto
2 tazas arroz
2 cucharadas aceite vegetal
1 pequeña cebolla picada (como media taza)
1 diente de ajo, picado finamente

2 chiles poblanos, rostizados, pelados, sin semilla, desvenados y picados
2 tazas granos de maíz o un paquete de 280 gramos de granos de maíz congeladosó una lata de granos de maíz drenados.
1½ tazas Crema Agria Preparada (receta abajo)
227 gramos queso "Cheddar," rallado

Hervir el agua en una cazuela mediana, sobre fuego alto y agregar la mantequilla y sal. Cuando la mantequilla se ha derretido agregar el arroz y hervir. Reducir el fuego a bajo y cubra la cazuela y cocine por 20 minutos. Retire el arroz de la cazuela y esparza sobre una hoja de hornear para que se enfríe, o déjelo que se enfríe en la misma cazuela y cubrálo.

Mientras tanto pre-caliente el horno a 350 grados F (si usa un plato de Pyrex para hornear, ponga el horno a 325 grados F). Caliente el aceite en un sartén sobre fuego mediano hasta que esté caliente pero sin quemarlo. Reduzca la llama a mediano, agregar la cebolla y ajo y cocine, mezclando hasta que esté dorado, de 2 a 3 minutos. Agregar los chiles poblanos y cocine mezclando por un minuto. Deje que enfríen y despues combine con el arroz. Mezcle el maíz y la crema agría preparada, y el queso rallado.

Ponga la mezcla en un recipiente de hornear o cacerola y hornee hasta que se se haya celentado, como unos 30 minutos.

SIRVE 6

PARA LA CREMA AGRIA PREPARADA:

2 tazas crema agria cultivada
1 cebolla pequeña finamente picada (como media taza)
1 pequeño diente de ajo picado finamente
2 cucharadas cilantro finamente picado
Sal al gusto

Combine todos los ingredientes y deje que repose cinco minutos para que los sabores se combinen.

GENERA 2 TAZAS

ADOBE DE CHILE COLORADO (RED CHILE ADOBO)

(ADAPTED FROM *FOOD FROM MY HEART*, MACMILLAN, 1992)

2 tablespoons lard or vegetable oil
4 medium hot whole dried red chilies,
    either ancho, guajillo, or dried Anaheim,
    stems intact
1½ cups boiling water

1 large garlic clove, peeled and finely
    minced
1 teaspoon dried Mexican oregano
1 cup water

Heat the lard or oil in small or medium-size heavy skillet over medium heat, until rippling. Fry the whole chilies, one at a time, turning several times with tongs, until puffed and red or slightly orange in color, 30 to 60 seconds. Be careful not to let them burn! As the chilies are done, add them to the boiling water in a bowl. Let soak until softened, about 20 minutes. Push them down if they float. Drain. Pull or cut off the chili tops and scrape out the seeds. Discard the tops and seeds.

Place the soaked chili pods in a blender with the garlic, oregano, and 1 cup water. Process to a smooth puree. Add a little more water if desired to facilitate blending, but the sauce should be thick.

Place a medium-mesh sieve over the bowl. Pour the paste into the sieve and force it through with a wooden spoon, scraping and rubbing to push through as much of the solids as possible. Discard any bits that won't go through.

YIELDS 1 CUP

(DEL LIBRO *FOOD FROM MY HEART*, MACMILLAN, 1992)

2 cucharadas manteca o aceite vegetal
4 chiles rojos enteros, o chile ancho,
    guajillo, o Anaheim seco, con los tallos
    intactos
1½ tazas agua hirviendo

1 diente grande de ajo, pelado y
    finamente picado
1 cucharada orégano Mexicano seco
1 taza agua

Caliente la manteca o aceite en un sartén mediano sobre fuego medio hasta que se vean pequeñas olas. Fría los chiles enteros uno a uno, volteándolos regularmente con unas pinzas, hasta que el color rojo haya cambiado ligeramente y se hayan esponjado, 30 a 60 segundos. ¡Cuide de que nos se quemen! Ya que estén los chiles listos agréguelos al agua hirviendo y déjelos que se hablanden por unos 20 minutos. Empújelos al fondo si tienden a flotar. Escúrralos y corte la punta para sacar las semillas. Tire las puntas y las semillas.

Ponga las cáscaras de chile en una batidora con el ajo, orégano y una taza de agua. Procese hasta que obtenga un suave puré. Agregue mas agua si desea para facilitar batirlos, la salsa deberá de verse espesa.

Cuele el puré de chile y fórcelo con una cuchara y descarte los sobrantes que quedan atrapados en la coladera.

PRODUCE 1 TAZA

Luis Miguel

I'VE TRAVELED THE ENTIRE WORLD SINCE MY CHILDHOOD. HAVING A FATHER FROM SPAIN AND A MOTHER FROM ITALY HAS AFFORDED ME THE OPPORTUNITY TO EXPLORE DIFFERENT GASTRONOMIC ADVENTURES.

THESE RECIPES ARE INTERNATIONAL AND TWO OF MY FAVORITES.

BUEN PROVECHO!

LANGOSTA TERMIDOR ESPECIAL (SPECIAL LOBSTER THERMIDOR)

FOR THE BÉCHAMEL SAUCE:
6 tablespoons (3 ounces) butter
6 tablespoons all-purpose flour
1 cup milk
1 cup cream
3 tablespoons English mustard

FOR THE LOBSTER:
3 pounds large lobsters (without the shell)
⅓ cup oil
5 tablespoons butter
2 small cups cognac
20 thin slices truffle (imported French mushrooms)
20 ounces grated Parmesan cheese

To make the sauce, melt the butter in a saucepan over medium heat. Add the flour and stir until mixture begins to bubble, about 1 minute. Cook to remove the raw flour taste, but do not let darken past a light gold. Remove pan from heat. Using a whisk, blend in the milk, then the cream. Return pan to heat and continue whisking until sauce thickens and boils and has a smooth consistency, about 3 minutes. Whisk in the mustard. Remove from heat and strain.

In a skillet, sauté the lobsters with oil and butter. Cook for 4 minutes, add the cognac, and flame. Keep on the flame for 1 minute. Pour the sauce over the lobster, add the sliced truffles, and sprinkle with the Parmesan cheese.

SERVES 10

PARA LA SALSA BÉCHAMEL:
85 gramos mantequilla
85 gramos harina
¼ litro leche
¼ litro crema
50 gramos mostaza Inglesa

PARA LAS LANGOSTAS:
1½ kilogramos langostas grandes sin cáscara
80 mililtros aceite
70 gramos mantequilla
2 tazas (pequeñas) coñac
20 laminas trufa muy delgadas
570 gramos queso Parmesano, rallado

Para hacer la Salsa Béchamel, derritir la mantequilla en un sartén sobre fuego mediano. Añadir la harina y mezclar hasta hacer burbujas, como 1 minuto. Cocine para remover el sabor a harina cruda, pero no deje que se obscurezca mucho. Quite la cacerola del fuego y continúe mezclado hasta que espese y la mezcla hierva hasta tener una consistencia lisa, más o menos 3 minutos. Retirar del fuego y agregar la mantequilla y la mostaza. Quitarla del fuego. Colarlo.

En un sartén con aceite y mantequilla, freir las langostas. Dejar cocer durante 4 minutos, agregar el coñac y flamear. Dejar un minuto en el fuego. Echar la salsa sobre las langostas, añadir las láminas de trufa y espolvorear con el Parmesano.

SIRVE 10

SUFLE DE SALMÓN "DIVA" (SALMON "DIVA" SOUFFLE)

2 cups crabmeat
3 cups cream
6 pastry tart shells (pre-made)
1 cup cooked salmon
4 tablespoons butter
3 cups Béchamel Sauce (see recipe on previous page)
Salt and black pepper
2 egg whites
4 egg yolks

In a saucepan over medium heat, cook the crabmeat with the cream until heated through. Place in the bottom of the pastry shells. Mince the salmon and, in a saucepan, heat butter, then add salmon and Béchamel Sauce. Season with salt and pepper. Once the mixture is heated through, remove from heat. Beat egg whites with egg yolks until stiff. Add to salmon mixture, but do not overmix as to retain light texture. Mound salmon mixture over crab mixture on tart shells. Set oven to medium (350 degrees) and cook until done.

SERVES 6

---

500 gramos carne de cangrejo
3 tazas crema
6 tartaletas para rellenar
250 gramos salmón cocido
4 cucharadas mantequilla
600 mililitros Béchamel
Sal y pimienta
2 claras de huevo
4 yemas de huevo

Preparar una mezcla de cangrejos con la crema y ponerlo en el fondo de las tartaletas, completar con el salmón picado muy fino al que se agregan la mantequilla mezclado con Béchamel. Sazonar con sal y pimienta. Calentar la masa y retirar del fuego. Incorporar las yemas y claras batidas a punto de nieve. Cocer el horno moderado, a 350 grados F, hasta que esté cocinado.

SIRVE 6

Ricardo Montalban

IT'S PRACTICALLY IMPOSSIBLE FOR ME TO CHOOSE MY FAVORITE MEXICAN DISH. THE VARIETY OF MEXICAN CUISINE MIGHT BE EVEN GREATER THAN THE CHINESE. BUT, AS A CHILD IN MY HOME TOWN OF TORREON, COAHUILA, WE HAD A COOK WHO BECAME PART OF OUR FAMILY. LOLA WAS HER NAME. I CAN STILL SMELL THE AROMA EMANATING FROM THE KITCHEN, AND EVEN RIGHT NOW, AS I'M WRITING THESE WORDS, I FIND THAT I AM SALIVATING THINKING OF THE CHICKEN ENCHILADAS, NORTEÑO STYLE.

I HOPE YOU ENJOY THEM!

CHICKEN ENCHILADAS, NORTEÑO STYLE

2 chicken breasts
Salt to taste
4 ounces (two 2-ounce bags) of chilies guajillos
2 ounces (one 2-ounce bag) of chilies anchos
1½ ounces (¾ of a 2-ounce bag) chilies negros
1 head garlic
Pinch sesame seeds

5 small peppercorns
15 cloves
Pinch ground cumin
1 cup oil
¼ onion
12 corn tortillas
Mexican cheese
¼ head lettuce, shredded
½ cup sour cream

Place the chicken in water (with salt to taste) in a large saucepan. Cover and simmer until chicken is tender, about 20 minutes. Remove and shred the chicken, reserving the stock.

Toast all the chilies over an open flame until they blister. Let cool, remove the seeds and membranes, and soak chilies in cold water for 2 hours. In a deep frying pan, toast garlic, sesame seeds, peppercorns, cloves, and cumin separately, then put in a blender. Blend little by little to make sure it is well blended. Heat 2 tablespoons of the oil in a skillet, add the onion, and sauté until transparent. Remove the onion from skillet. Put the blended ingredients in the hot oil (you must stir constantly; if it thickens, you may thin with chicken broth) until boiling. Reduce heat and add salt to taste. In a skillet, heat ½ cup of oil. Add one tortilla at a time to the skillet. Remove once soft and dip in the sauce. Divide chicken evenly to make 12 enchiladas, then place enough chicken in the middle of each softened tortilla and roll up. In a baking pan, assemble enchiladas into rows. Top with any extra sauce and cheese. Bake in 350-degree oven until cheese melts. Garnish with lettuce and sour cream.

SERVES 4

ENCHILADAS DE POLLO ESTILO NORTEÑO

2 pechugas de pollo
Sal al gusto
100 gramos chiles guajillos
50 gramos chiles anchos
40 gramos chiles negros
1 ajo
Pizca semilla de ajonjolí
5 granos de pimienta

15 clavos de especia
Pizca comino
1 taza aceite
¼ cebolla
12 tortillas de maíz
Queso Mexicano
¼ lechuga
½ taza crema agria

Ponga el pollo en agua, sal al gusto y poner en un sartén. Tapar y hervir hasta que el pollo se ablande, como 20 minutos. Quitar y cortar el pollo, separe el caldo.

Cocinar los chiles sobre un fuego libre hasta que abran. Dejar enfriár, quitar las semillas y ponerlos en agua fría por dos horas. En un sartén hondo, freir el ajo, semillas de ajonjolí, granos de pimienta, clavos de especia y comino, separarlo, y despues poner en la batidora. Batir poco a poco hasta que esté bien batido. Calentar 2 cucharas de aceite en un sartén, añadir la cebolla y cocinar. Remover la cebolla del sartén. Poner la mezcla batida en el sartén, mezclando constante hasta hervir. Bajar el fuego y añadir sal al gusto. En otro sartén, calentar ½ taza de aceite. Poner una tortilla. Remover cuando se ponga suave y poner en la salsa. Deshebrar el pollo para hacer 12 enchiladas, poner en el centro de las tortillas, y enrollar. Poner en otra cazuela, distribuir el queso encima, y poner en el horno a 350 grados hasta que el queso se derrita. Agregar lechuga y crema agria.

SIRVE 4

Ricardo
Montalban

THIS RECIPE IS FROM A SPECIAL PERSON AND DEAR FRIEND OF MINE, ED LIEB. IT WAS CREATED BY DAFNA MORDECAI, WHO APPEARS SHARING HEALTHY RECIPES ON A NEW YORK–BASED CABLE PROGRAM TITLED *ACCENT ON WELLNESS.* ED HAS BECOME MY MENTOR ON MATTERS OF NATURAL HYGIENE AND HEALTH IN GENERAL.

IF PEOPLE ATE FOOD THE WAY IT WAS DESIGNED FOR THEM BY GOD OR NATURE, THEN WE'D BE A LOT BETTER OFF. THIS PIE RETAINS ALL OF THE NATURAL INTEGRITY PROVIDED BY THE GRACE AND NATURE THAT BROUGHT IT HERE. ALL WE NEED TO SURVIVE ARE RAW FRUITS AND VEGETABLES WITHOUT HUMAN PROCESSING. THERE'S SO MUCH LIFE IN THIS RECIPE...SO MUCH NATURE.

THAT'S WHAT IT MEANS TO ME—LIFE AND HEALTH—AND IT TASTES SO DAMN GOOD!

PASTEL DE FRUTA (NO-BAKE HEAVENLY FRUIT PIE)

2 cups raw nuts and seeds (I prefer to use walnuts, pecans, sunflower seeds, pumpkin seeds, and sesame seeds, but almost any combination of nuts and seeds will work.)

1½ to 2 cups dried fruit (dates, figs, raisins, prunes, apricots)

2 pounds ripe bananas (if possible, use several varieties, i.e., yellow, red, niños)

2 or 3 ripe mangoes (The fatter "yellow banana" mangoes are best. If fresh mangoes are not available, dried mangoes may be used if they are first soaked in water and reconstituted.)

1 pint ripe strawberries

2 kiwifruits

To form the crust, combine the nuts, seeds, and dried fruit in a Vitamix or food processor and press the resulting mixture into a 9-inch pie plate.

Cut the bananas lengthwise and cover the bottom of the pie about ½ inch deep. Pack down tightly using the back of a large serving spoon. Cover the banana layer with a layer of mangoes. Slice enough strawberries to cover the mango layer with a layer of strawberries.

(Optional: If your pie plate is deep enough and you have the patience, cover the strawberry layer with a second layer of bananas. This layer can be difficult to arrange.)

Garnish with the remaining strawberries and the kiwi slices.

SERVES 6

2 tazas nueces y semilla (cualquier combinacion: nueces, semillas de calabaza, girasol, ajonjolí)

1½ a 2 tazas fruta seca (pasas, higos, albaricoque, ciruela pasa)

1 kilogramo plátanos maduros (si es posible, usar una variedad, eje. amarillos, rojos, niños)

2 o 3 mangos maduros (si maduros frescos no son obtenibles, usar los secos pero remojarlos previamente)

2 tazas fresas maduras

2 frutas kiwi

Combinar las nueces, semillas y frutas secas en una batidora, batir y poner en el fondo del plato (23 centímetros para tartas), haciendo una pasta.

Cortar los plátanos a lo largo y cubrir el fondo del plato para tartas 1¼ centímetros. Con una cuchara, enpaquetar la fruta. Luego sigue con un nivel de mango, continua con un nivel de fresas. Si tienes espacio, otro nivel de plátanos.

(Opcional: Si su plato es lo suficientemente hondo y tiene paciencia, cubra la capa de fresas con una segunda capa de plátanos. Puede ser un poco más complicada esta capa.)

Decorar con fresas y fruta kiwi.

SIRVE 6

PICADILLO

¼ cup annato oil*
1 large onion, finely chopped
1 large green bell pepper, seeded and
    finely chopped
2 cloves garlic, finely chopped
1 fresh hot red or green pepper, seeded
    and chopped**
2 pounds ground round steak (or 1 pound
    ground sirloin, 1 pound ground pork loin)
2 large tomatoes, peeled and chopped,
    about 2 cups

½ teaspoon ground cumin
Pinch salt (careful—the olives and capers
    fulfill salt needs)
Fresh ground black pepper
½ cup seedless raisins
¼ cup pimiento-stuffed green olives,
    sliced
1 tablespoon capers
½ tablespoon fresh cilantro

Heat the annato oil in a large frying pan and cook the onion, bell pepper, garlic, and hot pepper until the onion is tender but not brown. Add the meat and cook, stirring and breaking it up until it has lost its color. Add the tomatoes, cumin, and salt and pepper to taste. Add the raisins, mix thoroughly, and simmer gently, uncovered, until cooked (about 20 minutes). Add the olives and capers and cook for a few minutes longer. Serve with plain boiled white rice, black beans, and fried sweet plantains.

SERVES 6

*To make annato oil, go to a Spanish grocery store and buy a package of annato seeds. Sometimes called achiote seeds, they are small and orange in color. Put a tablespoon of seeds in a frying pan with about ½ cup of any kind of oil you like (olive oil is good), and heat the oil until the seeds turn the oil a rust color. (BE CAREFUL! Annato seeds can jump out of the skillet and burn you if the burner is set too high.)

**If you find the Puerto Rican asicitos dulces, use 4 or 5 chopped. They look very much like scotch bonnets (also known as habaneros), but are not lethally hot like the bonnets. (Available in most supermarkets or Latino grocery stores, this ingredient is most important because it imparts a specifically Caribbean flavor.)

Rita Moreno

THIS WONDERFUL, FLAVORFUL DISH BRINGS BACK MEMORIES OF MY CHILDHOOD. WE WERE POOR, BUT WE ALWAYS ATE WELL. I REMEMBER MY MAMA PREPARING IT AND RECRUITING ME TO SLICE THE OLIVES. THE ENTIRE HOUSE WAS RESONANT WITH GORGEOUS SMELLS!

I INDICATE THAT THE RECIPE SERVES SIX—BUT IN THOSE DAYS, WE WOULD STRETCH THE DISH BY UTILIZING MORE RICE, BEANS, AND PLANTAINS.

IT'S A COLORFUL, AROMATIC, AND EXOTIC DISH—JUST THINK OF THE COMBINATION OF SWEET, SALTY, AND GARLICKY!

IT'S A GREAT COMPANY DISH THAT ONLY IMPROVES IF YOU MAKE IT ONE OR TWO DAYS BEFORE AND REFRIGERATE, BUT DON'T OVERCOOK IT WHEN YOU REHEAT!

BUEN APETITO!

PICADILLO

¼ taza aceite annato*
1 cebolla grande, cortada fina
1 aji verde grande, desemillado y cortado finamente
2 dientes de ajo, cortado finamente
1 aji verde o rojo picoso, desemillado y cortado**
1 kilogramo carne de res (picadillo o 500 gramos carne res, 500 gramos cerdo)

2 tomates grandes, pelado y cortado, como 2 tazas
½ cucharita comino
Pizca sal
Pimienta
½ taza pasas sin semilla
¼ taza aceitunas con pimientos, cortadas
1 cuchara alcaparras
½ cuchara cilantro fresco

Calentar el aceite annato en un sartén hondo y cocinar la cebolla, ají, ajo y ají picoso hasta que la cebolla esté blanda. Añadir la carne y cocinar, mezclando y separando la carne hasta que pierda el color. Añadir los tomates, comino y sal y pimienta a gusto. Añadir las pasas, mezclar y hervir poco, destapado hasta estar cocido, como 20 minutos. Añadir las aceitunas y alcaparras y cocinar unos minutos más. Servir con arroz blanco, frijoles negros y platanos maduros.

SIRVE 6

*Para hacer el aceite de annato, compra un paquete de semillas de annato. A veces lo llaman semillas de achiote. Son pequeños y de color naranja. Poner una cucharada de las semillas en un sartén con ½ taza de su aceite favorito y cocinar hasta que las semillas tengan un color rojo obscuro. (¡Cuidado: Si tiene el fuego muy alto, las semillas saltan del sartén y se puede quemar!)

** Si encuentra los asicitos dulces puertorriqueñes, use 4 o 5 picados. Se parecen a los habaneros, pero no son tan picantes. (Los puede encontras en la mayoría de los supermercados Latinos, este ingrediente es sumamente importante porque le da un toque específicamente Caribeño.)

Rita Moreno

Edward James Olmos

FRIJOLES DE LA OLLA

1 bag dried pinto or Roman beans (or 1 large can of pinto beans)
3 cloves garlic, finely chopped
1 large white or yellow onion
1 bunch cilantro, finely chopped
2 chicken bouillon cubes
1 tablespoon ground celery seed
1 packet Goya Sazon seasoning
3 strips bacon, finely chopped
1 ripe peach, cut into bite-sized pieces
1 serrano or jalapeño chili, seeded
Salt and black pepper to taste
1 lemon or lime
Tortillas

If using dried beans, sort and rinse in cold water. Put washed beans in a large pot and cover with 4 inches of water. Boil beans for 10 minutes in salted water. Take off heat. Add 2 more cups of water, cover, and let soak overnight. (If using canned beans, omit this step.)

Put soaked beans over medium heat and add garlic. Cut the onion in half and place one half into the pot. Cut the remaining half into two quarters and finely dice one of the quarters. Add the diced onion to the pot, reserving the remaining quarter for garnish. Add the cilantro, bouillon cubes, celery seed, Sazon, bacon, peach, and chili and let simmer for 2 to 3 hours. (If you use dried beans, the simmering time is closer to 5 hours.)

Add salt and pepper to taste. Serve with warm tortillas and chop up lemon or lime wedges. Sprinkle with the reserved onion and throw the lemon or lime rinds right in the bowl!

SERVES 4

---

1 paquete frijoles secos pinto o Romano (o una lata grande de frijoles pintos)
3 dientes de ajo, cortados finamente
1 cebolla blanca o amarilla
1 manojo cilantro, cortado finamente
2 cubos de bouillon de pollo
1 cucharada semilla de apio
1 paquete Sazón Goya
3 rajas tocino, cortado fino
1 melocotón maduro, cortado
1 chile Serrano o jalapeño, sin semilla
Sal y pimienta al gusto
1 limón o lima
Tortillas

Si está usando frijoles secos, lavar en agua fría. Poner frijoles lavados en una cazuela grande y cubrir con 10 cetímetros de agua. Hervir por 10 minutos en agua salada. Remover del fuego. Añadir 2 tazas más de agua, tapar y dejar por una noche. (Si está usando frijoles de lata, puede omitir este paso.)

Poner los frijoles sobre fuego medio, añadir el ajo, la mitad de una cebolla entera, cortar otro ¼ de la cebolla fina y añadir (separar la ultima mitad para el adorno). Agregar el cilantro, bouillon de pollo, semilla de apio, sazón, tocino, melocotón, chiles y hervir por 2 o 3 horas. (Si está usando frijoles secos, cocinar por 5 horas.)

Agregar sal y pimienta al gusto. Servir con tortillas calientes y rodajas de limón o lima. Poner cebolla picada en la cazuela.

SIRVE 4

CAMARONES NEGROS (BLACKENED SHRIMP)

2 tablespoons Spanish olive oil
¼ cup fresh garlic, chopped
10 to 12 shrimp (shell on)
1 teaspoon cracked black pepper
1 teaspoon dried thyme
1 teaspoon crushed red or cayenne
    pepper

½ teaspoon salt
½ teaspoon sugar
½ teaspoon pimiento or jerk seasoning
½ cup chicken or fish stock
4 ounces Worcestershire sauce
½ cup Red Stripe (or any dark) beer
Butter

In a medium saucepan, heat the olive oil. Add the garlic and sauté until golden brown. Add the shrimp and spices and sauté for 30 seconds. You want the shrimp to be blackened. Add the chicken or fish stock and Worcestershire sauce.

    Remove shrimp from pan and set aside. Reduce sauce to 1 cup. You want to achieve a thick gravy consistency. Use the beer and butter to adjust for consistency.

SERVES 2

---

2 cucharadas aceite de oliva Española
½ taza ajo fresco, picado
10 a 12 camarones (con cáscara)
1 cucharadita pimienta molida
1 cucharadita tomillo seco
1 cucharadita pimienta cayenne,
    machacado
½ cucharadita sal

½ cucharadita azúcar
½ cucharadita pimiento o sazonador "jerk"
½ taza caldo de pollo o pescado
112 gramos salsa Worcestershire
½ taza cerveza "Red Stripe" (o cualquier
    otra marca)
Mantequilla

En una olla mediana caliente el aceite. Agregue el ajo y saltéelo hasta quedar dorado. Añada los camarones y especias y saltée por 30 segundos. Quiere que los camarones se doren bien. Agregue el caldo y la salsa Worcestershire.

    Saque los camarones y apártelos. Deje que la salsa se reduzca a una taza y que espese. Use cerveza y mantequilla para ajustar la consistencia.

SIRVE 2

Toribio Prado

MASTER CHEF TORIBIO PRADO, "THE PATRON SAINT OF CARIBBEAN AND CONTEMPORARY LATIN CUISINE," IS THE MAN RESPONSIBLE FOR INTRODUCING CARIBBEAN CUISINE TO SOUTHERN CALIFORNIA.

THE TENTH OF 14 CHILDREN, PRADO WAS BORN IN MEXICO BUT WAS RAISED IN LOS ANGELES, THE CITY HE CONSIDERS HIS OWN. DURING HIS TRAVELS IN HIS YOUNGER YEARS, TORIBIO FOUND HIMSELF DRAWING UPON MANY ETHNIC CUISINES TO CREATE A CULINARY STYLE ALL HIS OWN. "HE CREATED A NEW CUISINE," SAYS LOS ANGELES FOOD CRITIC BILL STERN. "HE CREATED A STYLE OF COOKING WHICH I WOULD DEFINE AS PAN-CARIBBEAN."

TORIBIO HAS BEEN ON THE LOS ANGELES RESTAURANT SCENE SINCE THE AGE OF 14, WHEN HE BEGAN WORKING IN THE KITCHEN AT THE "POWER LUNCH" SPOT HUGO'S IN WEST HOLLYWOOD. AT THE AGE OF 17, HE BECAME HEAD CHEF AT THE IVY AND LATER IVY AT THE SHORE, WHERE HIS BROTHERS AND

ARROZ DE COCO (COCONUT RICE)

2 medium-sized shallots, finely chopped
2 tablespoons olive oil
2 ounces unsweetened shredded coconut
3 ounces dried cherries or raisins
Salt to taste

2 bay leaves
2 cups long grain rice
2 cups bottled water
2 ounces coconut milk
1 ounce dry white wine

Sauté shallots in olive oil in an ovenproof saucepan over medium heat for approximately 1 minute. Add the shredded coconut, cherries or raisins, salt, and bay leaves and sauté for 20 seconds. Add the rice, water, coconut milk, and wine and bring to a boil. Remove pan from the burner and put it in the oven at 350 degrees for 30 to 45 minutes.

SERVES 2

---

2 cebollitas verdes (medianas) finamente
  cortadas
2 cucharadas aceite de oliva
55 gramos de coco rallado sin endulzar
82 gramos cerezas secas o pasas
Sal a gusto

2 hojas de laurel
2 tazas arroz de grano largo
2 tazas agua embotellada
55 gramos leche de coco
28 gramos vino blanco seco

Saltée las cebollitas en aceite de oliva en un sartén a fuego medio por 1 minuto más o menos. Añada el coco, cerezas o pasas, sal y hojas de laurel y saltée por 20 segundos. Agregue el arroz, agua, leche de coco y vino y déjelo hervir. Retire el sartén del fuego y métalo en el horno a 350 grados por 30 a 45 minutos.

SIRVE 2

Toribio Prado

SISTERS CONTINUE TO WORK TODAY. IN 1986, AT THE FAR EASTERN END OF MELROSE AVENUE IN SILVER LAKE, CHA CHA CHA WAS BORN—THE FIRST CARIBBEAN CUISINE IN THE CITY. SOON AFTER THE SUCCESS OF CHA CHA CHA, TORIBIO OPENED CAFÉ MAMBO, PRADO RESTAURANT, AND CHA CHA CHA ENCINO. SINCE THEN, TORIBIO HAS OPENED NEW CHA CHA CHAS IN LONG BEACH AND LA JOLLA, AND CAVA, A HIGH-CONCEPT SPANISH TAPAS RESTAURANT AND SUPPER CLUB. HIS LATEST VENTURE, CHA CHA CHICKEN GOURMET TO GO, IS A CARIBBEAN FAST-FOOD RESTAURANT IN SANTA MONICA.

TORIBIO HAS WON NUMEROUS CULINARY AWARDS AND HAS BEEN FEATURED IN FOOD AND STYLE PERIODICALS, INCLUDING HIS BEING SELECTED AS ONE OF THE 100 COOLEST PEOPLE IN LOS ANGELES BY BUZZ MAGAZINE. HE HAS ALSO BEEN FEATURED IN FOOD & WINE, BON APPETIT, GOURMET, L.A. STYLE, LOS ANGELES MAGAZINE, SI MAGAZINE, DETAILS, VOGUE, HOUSE AND GARDEN, ESQUIRE, THE LOS ANGELES TIMES, AND VARIOUS NATIONAL AND LOCAL TELEVISION SHOWS. THE NAME TORIBIO PRADO HAS BECOME SYNONYMOUS WITH INNOVATIVE CUISINE AND FOOD STYLING.

POLLO CHA CHA (CHA CHA CHICKEN)

2 10- to 12-ounce free-range chicken breasts
Juice of 1 lemon
Juice of 1 lime
2 large cloves garlic
2 small shallots, halved
½ cup dry cooking wine
¼ cup olive oil
3 stems cilantro (remove stems and break into pieces)
3 stems fresh oregano (remove stems and break into pieces)
3 stems thyme (remove stems and break into pieces)
3 stems fresh dill (remove stems and break into pieces)
Salt and black pepper

Tenderize chicken breasts by pounding them between two sheets of plastic wrap. Combine the remaining ingredients (except salt and pepper) in a bowl and marinate the chicken breasts overnight. The next day, remove the chicken from marinade and add salt and pepper to taste. Grill over a medium charcoal fire or an indoor grill. Serve with Tropicana Sauce (see recipe on next page).

SERVES 2

---

2 pechugas de pollo (300 gramos cada una) criadas libremente
Jugo de 1 limón
Jugo de 1 lima
2 dientes de ajo grandes
2 cebollitas verdes, a la mitad
½ taza vino seco de cocina
¼ taza aceite de oliva
3 tallos de cilantro, en pedazos
3 tallos de oregano fresco, en pedazos
3 tallos tomillo, en pedazos
3 tallos eneldo fresco, en pedazos
Sal y pimienta

Ablande el pollo golpeándolo entre dos hojas de plástico. Combine el resto de los ingredientes en un recipiente y marine las pechugas durante una noche. El próximo dia saque las pechugas del líquido y ponga sal y pimienta al gusto. Cocínelas en un asador de carbón o a la parilla. Sirve con Aderezo Tropicana (receta sigue).

SIRVE 2

ADEREZO TROPICANA (TROPICANA SAUCE)

1 papaya
Shallot (from Cha Cha Chicken marinade)
Garlic (from Cha Cha Chicken marinade)
1 tablespoon olive oil
½ cup chicken stock
½ teaspoon cumin

½ teaspoon sugar
Drop balsamic vinegar
2 large oranges (Valencia or Van Nuys), peeled, seeded, and sliced
Red cilantro leaves for garnish

Scoop out the inside of the papaya, remove seeds, and blend the papaya in a blender until smooth. Remove shallots and garlic from marinade and sauté in olive oil very lightly for 10 seconds. Add the blended papaya to the shallots and garlic. Add the remaining ingredients except for the orange slices. Reduce heat and add the oranges. Pour over Cha Cha Chicken and garnish with red cilantro leaves.

SERVES 2

---

1 papaya
Cebollita verde (de la salsa de la receta para el Pollo Cha Cha)
Ajo (de la salsa de la receta para el Pollo Cha Cha)
1 cucharada aceite de oliva
½ taza caldo del pollo

½ cucharadita comino
½ cucharadita azúcar
Unas gotitas vinagre balsámico
2 naranjas grandes (Valencia o Van Nuys), sin semillas, peladas y rebanadas
Hojas de cilantro rojo (para adorno)

Quite lo de adentro de la papaya, tirando las semillas, y bata en la batidora hasta que esté líquido. Saltée el ajo y cebollita en aceite por 10 segundos. Agregue la papaya al ajo y cebollita. Añada el resto de los ingredientes excepto las naranjas. Reduzca el fuego y agregue las naranjas. Sirva la salsa sobre el Pollo Cha Cha y decore con hojas de cilantro rojo sobre las pechugas.

SIRVE 2

GORDITAS WITH TINGA POBLANO

FOR SHREDDED PORK WITH CHORIZO AND CHIPOTLE CHILIES:

2 pounds pork shoulder

1 whole white onion, quartered

2 pounds red tomatoes

½ pound chorizo, casing removed

4 cloves garlic, chopped

2 whole white onions, chopped

¼ cup flat-leaf parsley, chopped

4 whole canned chipotle chilies in adobo, chopped

4 tablespoons chipotle adobo sauce

Salt and pepper to taste

Bring 3 quarts of water to a boil and add pork and quartered onion. Simmer meat for 1 hour. Remove the meat from liquid and cool. When the pork is cool enough to handle, shred the meat using two forks, scraping with the grain. Toast the tomatoes. Put them in a plastic bag to "sweat" for a few minutes to loosen skin, then peel, core, and chop. Sauté the chorizo for 5 minutes with the garlic, onion, and parsley, then add the shredded pork, tomatoes, chipotle chilies, and adobo sauce. Simmer 10 minutes, uncovered. Add salt and pepper to taste.

NOTE: This is the filling for gorditas. They are served best with a robust red wine or Mexican beer.

FOR THE GORDITAS MASA:

2 tablespoons vegetable shortening

1 pound fresh masa

½ teaspoon salt

¼ cup flour

1 teaspoon baking powder

Vegetable oil

Refried beans

Shredded lettuce

Salsa

Cotija cheese, crumbled

Using a mixer, whip the shortening, then add the masa, salt, flour, and baking powder. Mix together and let masa rest about 5 minutes before making the gorditas. Now we are going to take the "bake, then fry approach." Divide the dough into 12 pieces, then pat each into a circle about 3 to 3½ inches wide and a quarter inch thick. Place on a baking sheet in a 400-degree oven and bake until they have a nice crust on them. Meanwhile, heat vegetable oil in a frying pan, then pop the gorditas into the oil. They will puff up.

Slit the gorditas open. Stuff with beans, shredded lettuce, salsa, and the tinga poblano, and top with the crumbled cheese.

SERVES 12

Miguel Ravago

INTERNATIONALLY ACCLAIMED CHEF MIGUEL RAVAGO OF AUSTIN, TEXAS, IS THE EXECUTIVE CHEF AND PARTNER AT BERTRAM'S RESTAURANT AND BAR. LONG RECOGNIZED FOR HIS CELEBRATION OF THE FOOD IN INTERIOR MEXICO, MIGUEL OFFERS A FRESH INTERPRETATION OF THE CUISINE OF MEXICO AND TEXAS USING THE BEST AND FRESHEST REGIONAL PRODUCTS.

MIGUEL'S SIGNATURE PREPARATIONS INVOLVE COMPLEX RECIPES AND TECHNIQUES THAT YIELD SURPRISINGLY SIMPLE BUT ELEGANT RESULTS. HE LEARNED THEM FROM HIS GRANDMOTHER, A NATIVE OF SONORA, MEXICO, AS A YOUTH, AND CONTINUED TO POLISH THEM DURING HIS 25 YEARS IN THE RESTAURANT BUSINESS. IN THE YEAR SINCE HE LEFT FONDA SAN MIGUEL, MIGUEL HAS BEEN TRAVELING AROUND THE COUNTRY, CONSULTING FOR RESTAURANTS AND SERVING AS THE REPRESENTATIVE OF MEXICAN CUISINE AT THE JAMES BEARD HOUSE.

"AT BERTRAM'S, I'LL BE EXPLORING

Miguel Ravago

DISHES THAT ARE NEW TO AUSTINITES," NOTED MIGUEL. "BECAUSE THERE ARE SO MANY DIFFERENT KINDS OF DISHES IN HISPANIC TEXAS CUISINE, THERE WILL BE NO EMPHASIS ON ENCHILADAS OR TACOS ON THE MENU. AUSTINITES HAVE VERY DISCERNING PALATES, AND I WANT OUR GUESTS TO BE ABLE TO EXPERIENCE THE FULL RANGE OF FLAVOR AND NUANCE." THE RESTAURANT CONTINUES TO OFFER THE FINE MEATS, GAME, AND SEAFOOD THAT HAVE MADE IT PROMINENT.

MIGUEL'S COOKBOOK, *COCINA DE LA FAMILIA*, WRITTEN WITH MARILYN TAUSEND, WAS PUBLISHED BY SIMON & SCHUSTER IN NOVEMBER 1997 IN BOTH ENGLISH AND SPANISH.

GORDITAS CON TINGA POBLANO

PARA EL CERDO EN TIRAS CON CHORIZO Y CHILES CHIPOTLES:

1 kilogramo carne de cerdo
1 cebolla entera, partida en cuatro
1 kilogramo tomates rojos, tostados y pelados
225 gramos chorizo, sin la tripa
4 dientes de ajo, picados

2 cebollas, picadas
¼ taza perejil picado de hoja plana
4 chiles chipotles en adobo enlatados
4 cucharadas salsa de chipotles
Sal y pimienta al gusto

Deje hervir 3 litros de aqua y agregue el cerdo y los cuartos de cebolla. Déjela cocer por 1 hora. Saque la carne del líquido y déjela enfriar. Cuando pueda tocar el cerdo sin quemarse, hágalo tiras con 2 tenedores. Tueste los tomates. Póngalos en una bolsa de plástico para que "suden" unos minutos y se despegue la piel. Pélelos, quíteles el centro y píquelos. Saltée el chorizo por 5 minutos con el ajo, cebolla y perejil. Añada el cerdo, tomates, chiles y salsa. Déjelo cocinar por 10 minutos, sin tapar. Ponga sal y pimienta al gusto.

NOTA: Este relleno es para las gorditas. Es mejor si se sirve con un vino tinto robusto o cerveza Mexicana.

PARA LA MASA PARA LAS GORDITAS:

2 cucharadas manteca vegetal
454 gramos masa fresca
½ cucharadita sal
¼ taza harina
1 cucharadita polvo para hornear

Aceite vegetal
Frijoles refritos
Lechuga picada
Salsa
Queso Cotija desmoronado

Usando la mezcladora, comience batiendo la manteca, la masa, sal, harina y polvo para hornear. Mezcle todo y déjela reposar 5 minutos antes de hacer las gorditas. Divida la masa en 12 piezas y haga cada pieza en un círculo plano de 7½ a 9 centímetros de ancho y ⅗ centímetro de grueso. Póngalas, en una placa para hornear, en el horno a 400 grados F y hornéelas hasta que se endurezca un poco la parte de afuera. Mientras tanto, caliente el aceite vegetal en un sartén, fría las gorditas y normalmente se hincharán.

   Parta las gorditas a la mitad. Rellénelas con los frijoles, lechuga, salsa, la tinga poblano, ponga el queso Cotija encima.

SIRVE 12

TAMALES WITH SHRIMP AND SCALLOP CREAM SAUCE

FOR THE TAMALE:

15 ounces unsalted butter, softened

9 tablespoons sour cream

3 tablespoons paprika (optional)

2 teaspoons salt, or to taste

1 pound fresh white corn masa, very fine

2½ cups chicken broth, if needed

48 whole corn husks, use 2 for each
   tamale soaked

Using a mixer, beat the softened butter for about 5 minutes. Add the sour cream, paprika (optional), salt, masa, and chicken broth to desired consistency, but do not use all of the broth if not needed. Spread masa on 2 corn husks, fold over, and tie at both ends. Place in a steamer and cook for approximately 45 minutes.

FOR THE CHILI PASTE:

9 whole ancho chilies, stemmed and seeded

3 tablespoons rice vinegar

9 cloves garlic

1½ teaspoons dried Mexican oregano

¾ teaspoon salt

Place the chilies in a bowl, cover with boiling water, and let soak for 30 minutes. Drain. Transfer the chilies to a blender and add the vinegar, garlic, oregano, and salt. Blend until smooth and set aside. It should make about 12 tablespoons of paste.

FOR THE SHRIMP AND SCALLOP SAUCE:

9 tablespoons butter or olive oil

40 whole medium shrimp, peeled,
   deveined, tails intact

20 whole sea scallops, cleaned

¾ cup tequila

4½ cups heavy whipping cream

Salt and pepper to taste

Chopped Italian parsley for garnish

Melt the butter or oil in a large heavy skillet over medium heat. Add the shrimp and scallops and sauté until shrimp turns pink and the scallops are done, about 3 to 5 minutes. Remove the skillet from heat. Add the tequila and ignite with a wooden match. Be careful to stand back as the flame will be quite spectacular. Return to the heat and cook, stirring with caution, until the flames subside. Transfer the shrimp and scallops to a bowl, using a slotted spoon, and cover with foil to keep warm. Boil the remaining tequila in the pan for 1 minute until reduced. Lower the heat and add the cream to the skillet. Simmer until reduced to a sauce consistency, about 5 minutes, adding salt and pepper to taste.

Place four shrimp and two scallops with a spoon of cream sauce on each tamale at serving time. Sprinkle with chopped Italian parsley.

SERVES 24

TAMALES CON SALSA DE CAMARONES Y VENERAS

PARA EL TAMAL:

425 gramos mantequilla sin sal, suavizada
9 cucharadas crema agria
3 cucharadas paprika (pimentón)
   (opcional)
2 cucharaditas de sal, o al gusto

554 gramos masa fresca de maìz blanco,
   muy fina
2½ tazas caldo de pollo, si es necesario
48 hojas para tamal, use 2 para cada
   tamal, remojadas

Usando la batidora, bata la mantequilla por 5 minutos. Agregue la crema agria, pimentón, sal, masa y caldo hasta obtener la consistencia deseada, pero no use todo el caldo si no se necesita. Ponga masa en 2 hojas, doble y ate por los dos lados. Póngalos en una vaporera y cocine por más o menos 45 minutos.

PARA LA PASTA DE CHILE:

9 chiles anchos, sin tallo, sin semilla
3 cucharadas vinagre de arroz
9 dientes de ajo

1½ cucharaditas orégano Mexicano seco
¾ cucharadita sal

Ponga los chiles en un recipiente, cubra con agua caliente y déjelos remojar por 30 minutos. Quite el agua. Pase los chiles a una batidora, agregue el vinagre, ajo, orégano y sal. Bata hasta quedar liso y póngalo a un lado. Hará unas 12 cucharadas de pasta.

PARA LA SALSA DE CAMARONES Y VENERAS:

9 cucharadas mantequilla o aceite de
   oliva
40 camarones medianos enteros,
   pelados, desvenados, con las colas
20 veneras enteras, limpias

¾ taza tequila
4½ tazas crema (nata para montar)
Sal y pimienta al sabor
Perejil Italiano picado, para adornar

Derrita la mantequilla en un sartén grande a fuego medio. Agregue los camarones y veneras y saltée hasta que los camarones se pongan color de rosa y las veneras estén veneras hechas, 3 a 5 minutos. Quite el sartén del fuego. Agregue el tequila y encienda con una cerilla de madera. Cuidadosamente apártese. Devuelva esto al fuego y mueva todo hasta que las llamas se extingan. Transfiera los camarones y veneras a un recipiente usando una cuchara con rendijas y cubra todo con papel de aluminio para mantenerlo templado. Hierva el tequila restante en el sartén y redúzcalo por un minuto. Baje el fuego y agregue la crema al sartén y sigue hirviendo hasta que se haya reducido a la consistencia de una salsa, unos 5 minutos, y agregue sal y pimienta al sabor.

Ponga 4 camarones y 2 veneras con una cucharada de salsa en cada tamal a la hora de servir. Espolvoree perejil picado.

SIRVE 24

ENCHILADAS CON JAIBA

6 poblano chilies
3 tablespoons butter
4 tablespoons flour
2 cups chicken stock, heated
½ cup heavy cream
Salt to taste

16 corn tortillas
Oil for frying
1 pound crabmeat (preferably fresh)
2 cups sour cream
1 small white onion, minced
4 radishes, sliced

Roast the poblano chilies in a 400-degree oven, allow to steam in a plastic bag, and, once skins are loose, peel and seed them. Put four of the chilies in a blender and puree well. Cut the other two chilies in rajas (1-inch-thin strips). In a saucepan, melt the butter and add the flour. Cook together over low heat for 5 minutes, pour in the heated stock, slowly stirring with a whisk, and add the cream and the chilies mixture. Strain the sauce and season with salt.

Fry the corn tortillas lightly in oil. Mix the crabmeat, sour cream, and onion together, saving some of the onion for the garnish. Spoon about 2 ounces of the crabmeat on each tortilla and roll up the enchiladas. Place them in a lightly greased pan and bake at 350 degrees until they are hot. Remove the pan from the oven and spoon the poblano chili sauce over the enchiladas. Garnish with sliced radishes and remaining onions. Serve with steamed white rice.

SERVES 8

6 chiles poblanos
3 cucharadas mantequilla
4 cucharadas harina
2 tazas caldo de pollo, caliente
½ taza crema para batir
Sal al gusto
16 tortillas de maíz

Aceite para freír
454 gramos carne de cangrejo (fresca de preferencia)
2 tazas crema agria
1 cebolla pequeña, finamente picada
4 rábanos, rebanados

Ase los chiles poblanos en el horno a 400 grados F, déjelos sudar en una bolsa de plástico y en cuanto se despeguen las pieles, pélelos y quite las semillas. Ponga cuatro de los chiles en una batidora y hágalos puré. Corte los otros dos chiles en rajas. En una olla, derrita la mantequilla y agregue el harina. Cocine todo junto a fuego lento por 5 minutos, agregue el caldo, moviendo lentamente, agregue la crema y la mezcla de los chiles. Cuele la salsa y sazone con sal.

Fría las tortillas ligeramente en el aceite. Mezcle la carne de cangrejo, crema y cebollas, guardando un poco de cebolla para decorar. Ponga unas 55 gramos de la carne de cangrejo en cada tortilla y enrolle las enchiladas. Póngalas en un refractario ligeramente engrasado y hornee a 350 grados F, hasta que estén calientes. Quite el refractario del horno y ponga la salsa de chile sobre las enchiladas. Adorne con rábanos y cebollas. Sirva con arroz blanco.

SIRVE 8

Frederico Reyes

BORN IN SALINAS, CALIF., A SECOND-GENERATION MEXICAN AMERICAN WITH MANY RELATIVES STILL LIVING IN MEXICO CITY, FREDERICO REYES' COOKING CAREER BEGAN IN 1971 AT A PRIVATE GOLF COURSE IN SALINAS. AFTER MOVING TO CARMEL VALLEY AND WORKING IN SEVERAL RESTAURANTS, HE ATTENDED THE CULINARY ACADEMY IN SAN FRANCISCO. THERE HE CONTINUED TO WORK IN RESTAURANTS WHILE ATTENDING SCHOOL. UPON GRADUATION, FREDERICO MOVED TO SACRAMENTO, CALIF., AND EARNED A POSITION AT LUTREC WHILE FURTHERING HIS CULINARY KNOWLEDGE IN ITALIAN AND AMERICAN CUISINES BEFORE BECOMING CHEF AT CENTRO COCINA MEXICANA.

HE HAS COOKED FOR SUCH CELEBRITIES AS ANTHONY QUINN, CLINT EASTWOOD, AND RAYMOND BURR, AND HAS DONE COOKING DEMONSTRATIONS ON SUCH SHOWS AS *LIVE WITH REGIS AND KATHIE LEE.* FREDERICO IS CURRENTLY

WORKING WITH THE LATINO CHAMBER OF COMMERCE IN FILMING A COOKING SHOW DEDICATED TO MEXICAN HOLIDAY DISHES.

HE WANTS TO CONTINUE RESEARCHING HIS LATINO ROOTS TO GAIN FURTHER KNOWLEDGE OF THE MEXICAN CUISINE.

TACOS DE PESCADO (FISH TACOS)

12 fillets of fish (mahimahi, red snapper, halibut, etc., preferably a white fish that grills well, about 3 ounces each)
3 cups white cabbage, thinly sliced
½ cup medium red onion, thinly sliced
1 tablespoon cilantro, coarsely chopped

½ bunch radishes
Juice of 1 large lime
Salt to taste
12 corn tortillas (preferably fresh)
Habanero Salsa (see below)
Recado Rojo (see below)

Make the Habanero Salsa and the Recado Rojo, then marinate the fish fillets in the Recado Rojo for at least an hour or up to 4 hours. Combine the cabbage, red onion, cilantro, and radishes in a bowl, mix the ingredients together, and add the lime juice and salt to taste. The salad can be prepared 5 minutes before using. Start a wood fire in a barbecue grill. Oil the grill well, then place over medium-hot coals. Grill the fillets until they are slightly pink in the middle. Place the fillets on the warm corn tortillas, spoon a small amount of Habanero Salsa on each fillet, and place a small pile of the cabbage salad on each taco.

FOR THE HABANERO SALSA:

8 ounces tomatillos (remove the husks)
½ Habanero chili, minced, seeded, and deveined
1 tablespoon white onion, finely diced

1 teaspoon cilantro, chopped
¼ cup fresh lime juice
¼ cup fresh orange juice

Chop the tomatillos into a fine dice. Add the rest of the ingredients in a mixing bowl and combine well. Let stand for 1 hour to develop flavors.

FOR THE RECADO ROJO:

¼ cup achiote seeds (soaked in water overnight to soften)
1 teaspoon whole oregano
⅛ teaspoon whole cumin
3 whole cloves
3 whole allspice berries

9 whole peppercorns
3 cloves garlic
4 tablespoons corn oil
2 tablespoons cider vinegar
½ cup orange juice
2 tablespoons lime juice

In a *molcajete* (mortar and pestle), grind the achiote seeds to a powder. Add the five spices and grind. Add the garlic and grind to a puree, then add the oil, vinegar, and citrus juices and mix them together. Let stand for at least 2 hours.

MAKES 12 TACOS

TACOS DE PESCADO

12 filetes de pescado que se ase bien (mahimahi, red snapper, halibut, 85 gramos cada uno)

3 tazas repollo blanco, rebanado

½ taza cebolla roja, rebanada fina

1 cucharada cilantro picado

½ racimo rábanos

Jugo de 1 lima grande

Sal al gusto

12 tortillas de maíz (frescas de preferencia)

Salsa Habanero (ver abajo)

Recado Rojo (ver abajo)

Haga la Salsa Habanero y el Recada Rojo, después marine los filetes de pescado en el Recado Rojo por 1 a 4 horas. Combine el repollo, cebolla, cilantro y rábanos en un recipiente; mezcle los ingredientes; agregue la lima y sal al gusto. La ensalada se puede preparar 5 minutos antes de usarse. Empiece un fuego en una parrilla para barbacoas. Engrase la parrilla bien con aceite y póngala sobre carbón de tamaño mediano. Ase el pescado hasta que estén ligeramente rosas por el centro. Ponga el pescado en tortillas calientes. Ponga un poco de la salsa Habanero en cada filete y ponga un poco de la ensalada de repollo en cada taco.

PARA LA SALSA HABANERO:

228 gramos tomatillos

½ chile Habanero, picado sin semillas y desvenado

1 cucharada cebolla finamente picada

1 cucharadita cilantro picado

¼ taza jugo fresco de lima

½ taza jugo fresco de naranja

Pique los tomatillos finamente. Agregue el resto de los ingredientes en un recipiente y combínelos bien. Deje reposar por una hora.

PARA EL RECADO ROJO:

¼ taza semillas de achiote (remojadas durante la noche para suavizarlas)

1 cucharadita orégano entero

⅛ cucharadita comino entero

3 clavos enteros

3 pimientas de Jamaica entera

9 granos de pimienta enter

3 dientes de ajo

4 cucharadas aceite de maíz

2 cucharadas vinagre de manzana

½ taza jugo de naranja

2 cucharadas jugo de lima

En un molcajete, muela las semillas de achiote hasta obtener un polvo. Añada el resto de las especias y muélalas. Agregue el ajo y hágalo puré, agregue el aceite, vinagre, y jugos y mézclelos. Déjelo reposar por 2 horas, por lo menos.

HACE 12 TACOS

CAMARONES CON TEQUILA (SHRIMP WITH TEQUILA)

4 shots Herradura, silver tequila
3 tablespoons cilantro, chopped
1 tablespoon garlic, chopped
3 jalapeños, chopped
1 cup olive oil

Salt
3 pounds (9 prawns, 4 ounces per serving)
   Mexican prawns (36 to 40 count)
Juice of 1 lime

In a barbecue grill, start a wood fire for grilling. Combine all the ingredients except prawns and lime and mix well. Add the prawns and coat gently with the marinade for at least 15 minutes. While the shrimp are grilling, season with a squeeze of lime. Serve with fresh, warm corn tortillas and Cactus-Corn Relish.

FOR THE CACTUS AND CORN RELISH:

6 ears white corn, husks removed
3 large nopales (cactus paddles), lightly
   coated with olive oil
2 cups red onions, sliced 1/4 inch, coated
   with olive oil
6 serrano chilies

⅓ bunch cilantro, chopped
¼ cup extra virgin olive oil
¼ cup juice for pickled jalapeños
Salt
Lime juice to taste

Grill the corn, cactus, red onions, and chilies until lightly browned and cooked through. With a sharp knife, remove the kernels from the corn cob. Dice the cactus paddles into ½-inch pieces. Chop the serranos. Combine the corn, cactus, onions, chilies, cilantro, olive oil, and juice in a mixing bowl and fold gently. Season with salt and lime juice.

CAMARONES CON TEQUILA

4 copitas de tequila Herradura
3 cucharadas cilantro picado
1 cucharada ajo picado
3 jalapeños picados
1 taza aceite de oliva

Sal
1½ kilogramos camarones Mexicanos (36-40 por ½ kilogramo)
Jugo de 1 lima

En un asador, encienda el fuego. Combine todos los ingredientes excepto los camarones y la lima y mezcle bien. Agregue los camarones y cúbralos con la salsa por unos 15 minutos, mínimo. Mientras los camarones se asan, sazone con jugo de lima. Sírvalo con tortillas calientes y la salsa de nopales y maíz.

PARA LA SALSA DE NOPALES Y MAÍZ:

6 mazorcas de maíz blanco, sin las hojas
3 nopales, ligeramente cubiertos de aceite de oliva
2 tazas cebollas rojas, en rebanadas de ½ centímetro, cubiertas de aceite de oliva

6 chiles serranos
⅓ manojo cilantro
¼ taza aceite de oliva "extra virgen"
¼ taza jugo para jalapeños curtidos
Sal
Jugo de lima al gusto

Ase al maíz, nopales, cebollas y chiles hasta que estén ligeramente dorados y cocidos. Con un cuchillo filoso, quite los granos de las mazorcas. Corte los nopales en cubitos de 1½ centímetros. Pique los chiles serranos. Combine todo lo anterior en un recipiente y mézclelo ligeramente. Sazone con sal y jugo de lima.

Frederico Reyes

Chita Rivera

THIS IS A VERY FESTIVE DRINK THAT WAS CREATED AT THE CAST PARTY FOR THE ORIGINAL *WEST SIDE STORY* COMPANY. IT REMINDS ME OF GOOD FRIENDS, GOOD MUSIC, AND A GOOD TIME.

CHITA'S MARGARITAS

8 ounces concentrated limeade (lime juice)
8 ounces tequila
8 ounces beer
½ large mango

Combine all the ingredients in a blender and blend. Pour into a fun, unique glass. No salt is necessary.

MAKES 1 MARGARITA

---

250 gramos jugo de limón verde concentrado
250 gramos tequila
250 gramos cerveza
½ mango grande

Mezclar todos los ingredientes en la batidora. Poner en un vazo alegre y singular. No se necesita sal.

HACE 1 MARGARITA

ARROZ CON HABICHUELAS
(PUERTO RICAN RICE WITH RED BEANS)

3 cups rice (small, medium, or long grain)
1/4 pound Puerto Rican sausage
   (salchichón), cut into 1/2-inch pieces
2 tablespoons tomato paste
1 large clove garlic, diced
1 small onion, diced
2 envelopes Goya Sazon seasoning mix
1 teaspoon adobo seasoning

2 tablespoons cooking oil
1 small pepper, diced
8 small green olives
3 capers (alcaparrado)
2 1/2 cups water
Branch coriander
1 can (28 ounces) red beans

Wash rice and place in a pot of water. In another pot over medium heat, add all remaining ingredients except the red beans. Stir to combine and simmer for 5 minutes. Add mixture and beans to rice and cook at medium-high heat until water evaporates. Stir, reduce heat to low, and cover. Cook for about 30 minutes, stirring a couple of times, and making sure mixture doesn't burn.

SERVES 5 TO 6

Recipe of Hilda Rodriguez (Geraldo Rivera's office) for *GERALDO*.

---

3 tazaz arroz
115 gramos salchichón, cortado
   en trozos de 1 1/4 centímetros
2 cucharadas pasta de tomate
1 diente de ajo, picado
1 cebolla pequeña, picada
2 sobres Sazón de Goya
1 cucharita sazón de adobo

2 cucharadas aceite
1 ají verde, cortado
8 aceitunas verdes pequeñas
3 alcaparras
2 1/2 tazas agua
Hoja coriander
1 lata (800 gramos) frijoles rojos

Lavar el arroz y poner en una cazuela con agua. En otra cazuela sobre fuego medio, añadir todo los ingredientes menos los fríjoles. Mezclar y cocinar por 5 minutos. Añadir la mezcla y frijoles al arroz y cocinar a fuego medio/alto hasta que el agua se consuma. Mezclar, poner a fuego lento y tapar. Cocinar por media hora, mezclando unas cuentas veces, asegurando que no se queme.

SIRVE 5 A 6

Receta de Hilda Rodriguez (oficina de Geraldo Rivera) para *GERALDO*.

Geraldo
Rivera

MY FAVORITE DISH IS RICE AND BEANS. THE WONDERFUL TASTE AND SMELL OF IT REMINDS ME OF MY CHILDHOOD VACATIONS WITH MY PATERNAL FAMILY IN PUERTO RICO.

GUINEOS EN ESCABECHE (GREEN BANANA SALAD)

10 green bananas
2 envelopes Goya Sazon seasoning
2 roasted red peppers, cut in pieces
12 stuffed olives
1 tablespoon olive oil

1 tablespoon cooking oil
1 medium onion, sliced
2 bay leaves
A few drops of vinegar

Peel and boil the green bananas. Cook until tender but not too soft. When done, place the bananas in cold water to cool, then slice into ¼-inch circles. Combine the remaining ingredients and add to the bananas. Mix gently.

Enjoy at room temperature.

SERVES 6 TO 8

Recipe of Hilda Rodriguez (Geraldo Rivera's office) for *GERALDO*.

---

10 plátanos verdes
2 sobres Sazón Goya
2 aji rojo asado, cortado
12 aceitunas rellenas
1 cucharada de aceite de oliva

1 cucharada aceite
1 cebolla mediana, cortada
2 hojas de laurel
Gotas de vinagre

Pelar y hervir los guineos. Cocer hasta que esté blando, pero no mucho. Cuando estén hechos, poner los plátanos en agua fría para enfríar y cortar en circulos de ½ centímetro. Mezclar todos los ingredientes y añadir a los plátanos. Mezclar lijeramente.

Servir.

SIRVE 6 A 8

Receta de Hilda Rodriguez (oficina de Geraldo Rivera) para *GERALDO*.

THE ORIGINAL PLANTAIN-COATED MAHIMAHI

6 mahimahi or halibut fillets
 (7 to 8 ounces each)

Salt and black pepper to taste
Garlic plantain chips for garnish

FOR THE TAMARIND TARTAR SAUCE:
1 cup mayonnaise
2 tablespoons freshly squeezed lime juice
1 tablespoon grated onion

¼ cup green and black olives, diced
¼ cup tamarind juice

FOR THE FUFU:
6 slices bacon (about 6 ounces), diced
1 small onion, cut into ½-inch dice

3 ripe plantains, peeled and cut into
 1-inch cubes

FOR THE PLANTAIN CRUST:
4 cups canola oil for deep frying
4 green plantains, peeled and thinly
 sliced

1 cup all-purpose flour
4 eggs, lightly beaten

Place the mayonnaise, lime juice, onion, olives, and tamarind juice in a mixing bowl and mix well. Refrigerate.

To prepare the fufu, fry the bacon in a hot, dry skillet until crisp, 4 or 5 minutes. Transfer to a plate and set aside. Add the onion to the skillet and sauté for another 2 minutes. Remove from heat and let cool.

Bring a saucepan of water to a boil. Add the ripe plantains, reduce heat, and simmer until soft, about 15 minutes. Drain, transfer the plantains to a mixing bowl, and mash with a potato masher or fork. Add the sautéed onion and bacon and keep warm.

To prepare the crust, in a saucepan or deep fryer heat the oil to 350 degrees. Add the green plantain slices and fry until golden brown, 3 to 4 minutes. Remove the slices with a wire-mesh strainer or slotted spoon, drain on paper towels, and let cool.

Transfer the fried plantains to a food processor, process to a coarse grind, and put into a bowl. Place the flour and eggs in separate bowls.

Season the mahimahi fillets on both sides with salt and pepper and dredge on one side only, first in the flour, then in the egg, and finally in the ground plantains. Let dry for 1 to 2 minutes.

Strain the frying oil and transfer ¼ cup to a large, clean skillet. Over medium-high heat, fry the fillets, coated side first, for 4 to 5 minutes per side, depending on thickness.

Place the fufu on serving plates. Arrange the mahimahi on top of the fufu, and top each serving with 2 tablespoons of the tartar sauce. Garnish with the remaining ground plantains.

SERVES 6

Douglas Rodriguez

DOUGLAS RODRIGUEZ, EXECUTIVE CHEF AND OWNER OF PATRIA IN NEW YORK CITY AND AQUARELA IN SAN JUAN, PUERTO RICO, WAS BORN IN NEW YORK TO CUBAN PARENTS AND MOVED TO MIAMI IN HIS EARLY TEENS. HIS NATURAL AFFINITY FOR FOOD BECAME APPARENT AT THE TENDER AGE OF 14, WHEN HE LANDED HIS FIRST JOB IN A MIAMI BEACH KITCHEN. AFTER HIGH SCHOOL, HE ATTENDED JOHNSON AND WALES UNIVERSITY IN PROVIDENCE, R.I., AND THEN RETURNED TO FLORIDA TO PLY HIS CRAFT APPRENTICING AT SEVERAL SOUTH FLORIDA HOTELS, WHERE HE FINE-TUNED HIS KEEN INTEREST IN LATIN INGREDIENTS.

CHEF RODRIGUEZ HAS BEEN SETTING THE RESTAURANT SCENE ON FIRE WITH HIS *NUEVO LATINO* CUISINE FOR MORE THAN EIGHT YEARS—FIRST AT HIS CRITICALLY ACCLAIMED RESTAURANT YUCA IN CORAL GABLES, FLA., WHICH HE OPENED IN AUGUST OF 1989, AND THEN

Douglas Rodriguez

IN NEW YORK IN FEBRUARY OF 1994 WITH THE OPENING OF HIS PHENOMENALLY SUCCESSFUL THREE-STAR RESTAURANT PATRIA. IN MAY 1997, HE OPENED AQUARELA AT THE EL SAN JUAN HOTEL AND CASINO IN SAN JUAN, PUERTO RICO.

CHOSEN BY *NEWSWEEK* MAGAZINE AS ONE OF THE 100 AMERICANS WHO WILL INFLUENCE US ALL IN THE COMING MILLENNIUM, DOUGLAS IS CONTINUING TO BLAZE A TRAIL WITH *NUEVO LATINO* CUISINE AS AUTHOR OF THE BOOK *NUEVO LATINO*, PUBLISHED IN OCTOBER OF 1995, AND *LATIN LADLES*, PUBLISHED IN FEBRUARY 1998. A LATIN INGREDIENTS POSTER AND BOOK WILL FOLLOW. CHEF RODRIGUEZ RECEIVED THE CHEFS OF AMERICA AWARD IN 1991, AND CULINARY MASTER OF NORTH AMERICA IN 1994. AFTER BEING NOMINATED FOR RISING STAR CHEF THREE TIMES BY THE JAMES BEARD FOUNDATION IN NEW YORK CITY, HE WAS AWARDED THE COVETED HONOR IN 1996. HE HAS ALSO APPEARED ON NUMEROUS TV COOKING SHOWS AND HAS BEEN THE GUEST CHEF ON THE *TODAY SHOW* AND *LATE NIGHT WITH DAVID LETTERMAN*.

EL MAHIMAHI ORIGINAL CUBIERTO DE PLATANO

6 filetes de mahimahi (delfín) o de halibut (200 a 228 gramos cada uno)
Sal y pimienta al gusto

Rebanadas fritas de plátano con ajo, como decoración

PARA LA SALSA TÁRTARA DE TAMARINDO:
1 taza mayonesa
2 cucharadas jugo de lima fresco
1 cucharada cebolla rallada

¼ taza aceitunas verdes y negras, rebanadas
¼ taza jugo de tamarindo

PARA EL FUFU:
6 tiras de tocino (como 170 gramos) en cuadros
1 cebolla pequeña, en cubos de 1½ centímetros

3 plátanos maduros, pelados y cortados en cubos de 2½ centímetros

PARA LA CORTEZA DE PLÁTANO:
4 tazas aceite de canola, para freír
4 plátanos machos verdes, pelados y en rebanadas finas

1 taza harina
4 huevos, ligeramente batidos

Ponga la mayonesa, jugo de lima, cebolla, aceitunas y jugo de tamarindo en un recipiente y mezcle bien. Refrigere.

Para preparar el fufu, fría el tocino en un sartén caliente y seco hasta que quede crujiente, 4 a 5 minutos. Póngalo en un plato y póngalo a un lado. Agregue la cebolla al sartén y saltee por 2 minutos más. Quite del fuego y deje enfriar.

Hierva agua en una olla. Agregue los plátanos maduros, baje el fuego y deje hervir hasta que estén blandos, unos 15 minutos. Quite el agua y pase los plátanos a un recipiente y machaque con un machacador o un tenedor. Agregue la cebolla salteada y el tocino y mantenga caliente.

Para preparar la corteza, en una olla o freidora caliente el aceite a 350 grados F. Agregue las rebanadas de plátano y fría hasta quedar doradas, 3 a 4 minutos. Remueva las rebanadas con un colador, déjelas escurrir en toallitas de papel y déjelas enfriarse.

Pase el plátano frito a un procesador de alimentos, muélalos hasta quedar molido en trozos no muy pequeños y póngalo en un recipiente. Ponga el harina y los huevos en recipientes separados.

Sazone los filetes de mahimahi por los dos lados con sal y pimienta y pase primero por el harina después por el huevo y al final por los plátanos molidos, pero solamente por un lado. Déjelos secar por 1 a 2 minutos.

Cuele el aceite para freír y ponga ¼ de taza en un sartén grande y limpio. A fuego medio, fría los filetes, primero por el lado cubierto, por 4 a 5 minutos por lado, dependiendo del grosor.

Ponga el fufu en platos. Arregle el mahimahi encima del fufu y ponga 2 cucharadas de salsa tártara sobre cada plato. Decore con los trozos de plátano.

SIRVE 6

CHOCOLATE TRES LECHES

FOR THE CHOCOLATE MOUSSE:

7 ounces semisweet chocolate, chopped

¼ cup heavy cream

6 egg yolks

¼ cup sugar

1 tablespoon Grand Marnier or Cointreau (optional)

1½ cups heavy cream, whipped

NOTE: The mousse, which can also be made as a dessert all on its own, should be made a day ahead.

FOR THE CAKE:

1 cup all-purpose flour

¼ cup cocoa powder

1 teaspoon baking powder

½ teaspoon salt

5 eggs, at room temperature

1 cup sugar

⅓ cup water

2 teaspoons pure vanilla extract

FOR THE TRES LECHES:

1 can (12 ounces) evaporated milk

1 can (14½ ounces) condensed milk

1½ cups heavy cream

2 tablespoons Hershey's chocolate syrup

To prepare the mousse, in a double boiler melt the chocolate in the cream. Remove from heat and let cool slightly. With an electric mixer on high speed, beat the egg yolks and sugar in a mixing bowl until pale yellow and double in volume (or whisk vigorously over a water bath or double boiler until you achieve the same results). Quickly beat in the melted chocolate mixture all at once. Add the liqueur, if desired. Gently fold in the whipped cream until thoroughly incorporated. Place in the refrigerator and chill overnight.

The next day, preheat the oven to 400 degrees. To prepare the cake, sift the flour, cocoa powder, baking powder, and salt into a mixing bowl and set aside. In another mixing bowl, beat the eggs and sugar with an electric mixer on high speed for about 2 minutes. With the mixer running, add the water and vanilla all at once and continue beating until the mixture is a fluffy, pale yellow and double in volume, about 10 minutes.

Turn off the mixer and quickly fold in the reserved dry ingredients (if you take too long, the eggs will drop in volume). Pour the cake batter into a lightly buttered 13 x 9-inch cake pan and firmly tap the pan once or twice to remove any air bubbles.

Transfer the pan immediately to the oven and bake until a toothpick inserted comes out clean, about 10 minutes. Remove from the oven and let cool.

Meanwhile, whisk all of the tres leches ingredients together in a large mixing bowl until well blended. Run a knife around the edges of the cake pan and poke holes in the entire surface of the cake with a toothpick. Pour the milk mixture over the cake, 1 cup at a time, until the cake can't absorb any more liquid. Cover and reserve in refrigerator. Use any excess milk mixture for shakes.

To serve, cut the cake into pieces and spread the refrigerated mousse over each piece.

SERVES 12 TO 15

Douglas Rodriguez

CHOCOLATE TRES LECHES

PARA EL MOUSSE DE CHOCOLATE:

200 gramos de chocolate semi-dulce,
  picado
¼ taza crema para batir
6 yemas de huevo

¼ taza azúcar
1 cucharada Grand Marnier o Cointreau
  (opcional)
1½ taza crema para batir, batida

NOTA: El mousse, que también se puede preparar como postre por sí solo, se debe preparar un día antes.

PARA EL PASTEL:

1 taza harina
½ taza cacao en polvo
1 cucharadita polvo para hornear
½ cucharadita sal

5 huevos, a temperatura ambiental
1 taza azúcar
⅓ taza agua
2 cucharaditas extracto puro de vainilla

PARA LAS TRES LECHES:

1 lata (330 gramos) leche evaporada
1 lata (400 gramos) leche condensada
1½ tazas crema para batir

2 cucharadas jarabe de chocolate
  Hershey's

Para preparar el mousse, en una olla doble, derrita el chocolate en la crema. Quítelo del fuego y déjelo enfriar un poco. Con una batidora de mano a alta velocidad, bata las yemas y azúcar en un recipiente hasta que queden color amarillo pálido y se hayan duplicado en volumen (o bata vigorosamente sobre un baño de agua caliente hasta obtener los mismos resultados). Rápidamente bata el chocolate con las yemas, todo a la vez. Agregue el licor, si desea. Con cuidado mezcle la crema batida hasta que se haya incorporado totalmente. Ponga el refrigerador y enfríe durante la noche.

El siguiente día, precaliente el horno a 400 grados. Para preparar el pastel, cierna el harina, cacao en polvo, polvo para hornear y sal en un recipiente y póngalo a un lado. En otro recipiente bata los huevos y azúcar con una batidora eléctrica a velocidad alta por 2 minutos. Con la batidora encendida, agregue el agua y vainilla todo a la vez y continúe batiendo hasta que la mezcla esté esponjosa, amarilla pálida y duplicada en volumen, unos 10 minutos.

Apague la batidora y rápidamente incorpore los ingredientes secos (si tarda mucho los huevos perderán volumen). Vierta la mezcla para el pastel en un refractario de 33 x 23 centímetros ligeramente engrasado y con fuerza déle uno o dos golpecitos para quitar cualquier burbuja de aire.

Transfiera el refractario inmediatamente al horno y hornee hasta que al meter un palillo de dientes salga limpio, unos 10 minutos. Saque del horno y déjelo enfriar.

Mientras tanto, bata todos los ingredientes para las tres leches juntos en un refractario grande hasta que estén bien mezclados. Pase un cuchillo alrededor del refractario y haga agujeritos en la superficie completa con un palillo de dientes. Vierta la mezcla de la leche sobre el pastel, 1 taza a la vez hasta que el paste no pueda absorber más líquido. Cúbralo y guarde en el refrigerador. Use cualquier exceso de leche para batidos.

Para servir, corte el pastel en trozos y unte el mousse refrigerado en el pastel.

SIRVE 12 A 15

ENSALADA DE FRUTA TROPICAL (TROPICAL FRUIT SALAD)

1 whole pineapple
½ small papaya, chopped
½ mango, chopped
½ small mamey, chopped
1 kiwifruit, peeled, cut in half lengthwise,
   and sliced

5 strawberries, cut in half
1 tablespoon raisins for garnish
1 lime, sliced or cut in wedges for garnish
   and for sweetening fruit

TO PREPARE PINEAPPLE:

Hold the pineapple upright. Using an 8- or 10-inch chef's knife, slice the pineapple vertically 1 inch off the center of the fruit, leaving the leaves completely intact.

Lay the pineapple half on its side so that the cut part is facing up. With a small paring knife, trim around the fruit, leaving a 1-inch parameter. Scoop out the inside and save for the filling. Chop the fruit if necessary.

Fill the pineapple with the tropical fruits. Once the pineapple has been filled, sprinkle the raisins on top and place the lime on the rim. If desired, juice the lime over the fruit just before eating.

NOTE: Although tropical fruits are used in this recipe, a salad like this can be made with any combination of fruit. It is always recommended to use seasonal fruits, since they will be the freshest and tastiest.

SERVES 1

Cristina Saralegui

LIVING IN MIAMI, SUMMER CAN BE A BIT HEAVY, NOT TO MENTION MY WAISTLINE, SO MY TROPICAL FRUIT SALAD CAN BE A REAL LIFESAVER! SERVED VERY COLD, IT IS VERY REFRESHING. TRY IT. YOU'LL LOVE IT!

1 piña completa
½ papaya pequeña, cortada
½ mango, cortado
½ mamey pequeño, cortado
1 fruta kiwi, cortado por la mitad a lo largo,
   luego cortado en rayas

5 fresas, cortado por la mitad
1 cucharada pasas (reservar para adorno)
1 limón verde, cortado (reservar para
   adorno y para dulciar la fruta)

PARA PREPARAR LA PIÑA:

Retenerla parada, utilizando un cuchillo de chef de 20 o 25 centímetros, cortar la piña, 2½ centímetros del centro, dejando las hojas intactas.

Acostar la piña y cortar por el rededor dejando un grueso (espesor) de 2½ centímetros. Con una cuchara, sacar la fruta de la piña y retener para rellenar. Picarla si es necesario.

Llenar la piña con las frutas tropicales. Cuando la piña esté llena, poner las pasas encima, y poner el limón verde alrededor.

NOTA: Aunque yo utilicé frutas trópicales para ésta receta, se puede usar cualquier fruta fresca y refrescante. Siempre se recomiendan las frutas de la estación porque serán las más frescas y sabrosas.

SIRVE 1

CARNE ESTOFADA (BEEF STEW)

2 pounds of mixed cuts of beef
Garlic and salt for marinating
½ cup red wine
1 tablespoon salt
1 onion, diced
1 tablespoon lard
1 bell pepper, sliced
1 carrot, peeled and sliced (optional)
1 teaspoon garlic powder
1 tomato, peeled
1 bay leaf
½ cup peas (petit pois)

Marinate the meat the day before with wine, garlic, and salt. In a large pan over medium heat, sauté the onion in the lard until it is translucent. Add the bell pepper, carrots (optional), garlic powder, and the meat in small portions. Stir until the meat becomes brown, then add 1 cup of water, the tomato, and the bay leaf. Cover and cook until the meat is tender. Add the peas before serving, and allow stew to come back to a boil.

SERVES 4

---

1 kilogramo cortes variados de carne
Ajo y sal para sazonar
½ taza vino tinto
1 cucharada sal
1 cebolla, cortada
1 cuchara manteca
1 ají, cortado
1 zanahoria, pelada y cortada (opcional)
1 cucharita polvo de ajo
1 tomate, pelado
1 hoja de laurel
½ taza guisantes

Sazonar la carne el día antes con vino, el ajo y sal. En una cazuela grande sobre fuego medio, cocinar la cebolla en la manteca hasta que quede transparente. Añadir los ajíes, zanahoria (opcional), polvo de ajo y las carnes en porciones pequeñas. Mezclar hasta que la carne pierda su color, luego agregar una taza de agua, tomate y hoja de laurel. Tapar y cocinar hasta que la carne esté blanda. Añadir los guisantes antes de servir, dejando hervir de nuevo.

SIRVE 4

Jon Secada

THIS RECIPE WAS ONE OF MY DAD'S SPECIALTIES WHEN HE OWNED HIS RESTAURANT AND IT HAPPENS TO BE MY FAVORITE DISH.

Julian Serrano

JULIAN SERRANO IS CURRENTLY THE EXECUTIVE CHEF OF PICASSO BY SERRANO IN STEVE WYNN'S BELLAGIO HOTEL & RESORT IN LAS VEGAS. PREVIOUSLY HE WAS THE EXECUTIVE CHEF OF MASA'S, THE TOP-RANKED 65-SEAT, NATIONALLY AND INTERNATIONALLY ACCLAIMED FRENCH RESTAURANT, LOCATED ADJACENT TO THE HOTEL VINTAGE COURT IN SAN FRANCISCO.

A NATIVE OF MADRID, SPAIN, JULIAN IS A GRADUATE OF ESCUELA GASTRONOMIE P.P.O. HOTEL MANAGEMENT SCHOOL IN MARBELLA ON SPAIN'S COSTA DEL SOL. HE HAS WORKED IN SOME OF EUROPE'S MOST CELEBRATED KITCHENS, INCLUDING LUCAS-CARTON IN PARIS, HOTEL DE FRANCE IN AUCH, SOUTHWEST FRANCE, CHEZ MAX IN ZURICH, AND L'AUBERGINE IN MUNICH.

JULIAN BEGAN HIS WORKING RELATIONSHIP WITH MASA'S IN MAY OF 1984 WHEN HE WAS HIRED AND PERSONALLY TRAINED BY THE RESTAURANT'S

DUNGENESS CRAB WITH ARTICHOKE AND ORGANIC WHITE RAISINS

1 whole Dungeness crab
2 large artichokes
2 egg yolks
2 cups vegetable oil
Touch Tabasco sauce
Splash orange juice
1 teaspoon Worcestershire sauce
Splash cognac
1 tablespoon ketchup
Salt and black pepper
4 tablespoons mayonnaise
Organic white raisins
Lettuce (baby romaine, frisee, Bella Rosa)

In a large pot, bring salted water to a boil and add crab. A 3-pound crab should be cooked for 7 to 8 minutes. Remove crab and allow to cool. Clean crab, keeping the leg and claw meat intact and the meat from the body in a separate bowl. Set aside.

Clean, boil, and peel artichokes. Slice into ⅛-inch slices and then make ⅛-inch strips (batons). Cook artichokes in lightly salted water. When done, drain and cool. Set aside.

In a separate bowl, add the egg yolks and mix with vegetable oil to make mayonnaise. When done, remove half to another bowl. In the remaining mayonnaise, add Tabasco, orange juice, Worcestershire Sauce, cognac, and ketchup. Add salt and pepper to taste. This mayonnaise is Sauce Amercain.

In a bowl, add the artichoke, the crabmeat from the body, and 4 tablespoons plain mayonnaise. Mix gently together. Add salt and pepper to taste. Add raisins.

FOR THE PRESENTATION:
In the center of each plate, place one spoonful of artichoke and crab. On top of this, place nine pieces of crab leg and claw meat with a little Sauce Americain and a nice lettuce mélange. Design plate with more Sauce Americain.

SERVES 6

Julian Serrano

FOUNDING EXECUTIVE CHEF, MASA KOBAYASHI.

"MASA GAVE MY LIFE TO ME," JULIAN SAID. "I FINALLY REALIZED THAT I COULD BE A CREATIVE CHEF, THAT I COULD MAKE BEAUTIFUL THINGS WITH TALENTED PEOPLE, THAT I COULD STRIVE FOR PERFECTION."

JULIAN BECAME EXECUTIVE CHEF IN 1984, TAKING FRENCH CUISINE TO A NEW LEVEL BY USING THE FRESHEST INGREDIENTS, CLASSIC SAUCES, AND WORK-OF-ART PRESENTATION. UNDER HIS DIRECTION, MASA'S HAS WON THE SAN FRANCISCO FOCUS GOLD MEDAL AWARD FOR BEST RESTAURANT THE LAST 12 CONSECUTIVE YEARS. HE WON THE SAN FRANCISCO FOCUS CHEF OF THE YEAR AWARD IN 1994 AND WAS CHOSEN TO BE THE ONLY CHEF TO PREPARE DINNER FOR THE HIGHLY ACCLAIMED NAPA VALLEY WINE AUCTION IN 1995. JULIAN WAS ALSO NOMINATED BY THE JAMES BEARD FOUNDATION FOR BEST CHEF IN CALIFORNIA IN 1994, 1995, AND 1996. MASA'S WAS NOMINATED BY THE JAMES BEARD FOUNDATION FOR BEST RESTAURANT IN 1996. CHEF SERRANO HAS COLLABORATED WITH JULIA CHILD ON HER SHOW, *COOKING WITH MASTER CHEFS*, AND IN HER COOKBOOK. HE HAS ALSO APPEARED ON THE DISCOVERY CHANNEL ON *GREAT CHEFS IN GREAT CITIES*. BOTH SHOWS AIRED IN 1996.

CANGREJO CON ALCACHOFAS Y PASAS BLANCAS ORGÁNICAS

1 cangrejo entero
2 alcachofas grandes
2 yemas de huevo
2 tazas aceite vegetal
Poco de Tabasco
Poco de jugo de naranja
1 cucharadita salsa Worcestershire
Poco de coñac
1 cucharada salsa de tomate ketchup
Sal y pimienta negra
4 cucharadas mayonesa
Pasas blancas orgánicas
Lechuga (diferentes tipos)

En una olla grande, ponga agua salada, déjela hervir y agregue el cangrejo. Un cangrejo de $1^{1}/_{3}$ kilogramos puede ser cocido por 7 a 8 minutos. Quite el cangrejo y deje que se enfríe. Limpie el cangrejo, manteniendo la carne de las piernas y tenazas intacta y la carne del cuerpo en un recipiente apartado.

Limpie, hierva y pele las alcachofas. Rebane en rebanadas de $1/_{3}$ centímetro. Cueza las alcachofas en agua ligeramente salada. Cuando estén cocidas, quite el agua y enfríe. Ponga a un lado.

En un recipiente separado, agregue las dos yemas y mézclelas con el aceite y mayonesa. Cuando esté listo, ponga la mitad en otro recipiente. En el resto de la mayonesa agregue el Tabasco, salsa de tomate, coñac, jugo de naranja y salsa Worcestershire. Agregue sal y pimienta al gusto. Esta mayonesa es llamada Salsa Americana.

En un recipiente, agregue las alcachofas, la carne del cuerpo del cangrejo y 4 cucharadas de mayonesa natural. Mezcle todo junto. Agregue sal y pimienta al gusto. Agregue las pasas.

PARA LA PRESENTACIÓN:
En el centro del plato, ponga una cucharada de alcachofa y cangrejo. Sobre esto, ponga nueva piezas de cangrejo con un poco de Salsa Americana y lechuga. Decore el plato con Salsa Americana.

SIRVE 6

ROASTED LANGOUSTINES
WITH "PISTO" AND LEMON-BALSAMIC VINAIGRETTE

Olive oil
1 red bell pepper, cubed
1 small white onion, cubed
2 cloves garlic, peeled
1 yellow zucchini, cubed
1 green zucchini, cubed
Salt and black pepper

1 small Japanese eggplant, cubed and
    salted to absorb moisture (set aside for
    approximately 25 minutes)
2 langoustines, peeled, head removed,
    tail kept in shell
2 tablespoons olive oil

In a sauté pan over low heat, add the olive oil, red bell pepper, onion, and garlic. Cook very slowly, sweating vegetables to release juices. In a separate pan, sauté yellow and green zucchini in oil until half cooked. Drain oil, add salt and pepper. Add to garlic, pepper, and onion mixture. Sauté eggplant in oil. Drain oil and add to vegetable mixture. Set aside and keep warm. For langoustines, add 2 tablespoons olive oil to pan and sauté langoustines in curve of pan to form half moon shape.

FOR THE LEMON-BALSAMIC VINAIGRETTE:

3 tablespoons sherry vinegar
3/4 to 1 cup virgin olive oil
Juice of 1 whole lemon

Salt and black pepper
1 tablespoon good-quality balsamic
    vinegar

Put sherry vinegar in a deep bowl. Slowly add olive oil, lemon juice, salt, and pepper. Lastly, slowly add balsamic vinegar.

FOR THE PRESENTATION:

Place ½-inch ring-shaped mold on top portion of plate and fill with vegetables. Compress down and remove mold. Place langoustines on head and tail with head of langoustines meeting below vegetable presentation and each tail pointed toward lower opposite sides of plate. Drizzle plate with lemon-balsamic vinaigrette.

LANGOSTINOS ASADOS CON PISTO Y VINAGRETA BALSAMICA DE LIMÓN

Aceite de oliva
1 pimiento rojo, en cubitos
1 cebolla pequeña, en cubitos
2 dientes de ajo, pelados
1 calabacita amarilla, en cubitos
1 calabacita verde, en cubitos
Sal y pimienta

1 berenjena japonesa pequeña, en cubos y con sal para absorber la humedad (póngala a un lado por unos 25 minutos)
2 langostinos, pelados y sin la cabeza, deje la colita.
2 cucharadas de aceite de oliva

En un sartén a fuego lento, añada el aceite, pimiento, cebolla y ajo. Cuézalo lentamente, dejando que las verduras suelten los jugos. En un sartén aparte, saltée las calabacitas en aceita hasta que estén medio cocidas. Quite el aceite y agregue sal y pimienta. Agregue al ajo la mezcla de pimientos y cebolla. Saltée la berenjena en aceite. Quite el aceite y agregue la mezcla de vegetales. Póngalo a un lado y mantenga caliente. Para los langostinos, ponga aceite en un sartén y saltée los langostinos en la curva del sartén para darles la forma de media luna.

PARA LA VINAGRETA BALSÁMICA DE LIMÓN:

3 cucharadas vinagre de jerez
¾ a 1 taza aceite de oliva
Jugo de un limón

Sal y pimienta
1 cucharada vinagre balsámico de buena calidad

Ponga el vinagre de jerez en un recipiente hondo. Lentamente agregue el aceite de oliva, limón, sal y pimienta. Finalmente y despacio agregue el aceite balsámico.

PARA LA PRESENTACIÓN:

Ponga un molde redondo de $1\frac{1}{2}$ centímetros encima del plato y llénelo con verduras. Comprima y quite el molde. Ponga los langostinos a cabeza y cola con la cabeza debajo de las verduras y cada cola apuntando hacia la parte inferior del plato. Ponga un poco de la vinagreta en el plato.

Julian Serrano

MEDALLIONS OF VENISON WITH CARAMELIZED GREEN APPLES

1 saddle venison (2 ounces per medallion)
Extra virgin olive oil
1 tablespoon tomato paste
2 handfuls mire poix (rough dice of carrot,
   onion, celery, and leeks)
Bouquet garni (mix of thyme, bay leaf,
   parsley, leek, and celery tied in a
   cheesecloth bag)
2 shallots

2 cups red wine
½ cup port
Salt and black pepper to taste
6 tablespoons clarified butter
5 Granny Smith apples, sliced
2 tablespoons powdered sugar
18 baby carrots
36 asparagus tips

Debone and clean saddle. Reserve meat scraps and bone for sauce. Cut medallions to desired weight. Cut the bones into small pieces.

FOR THE SAUCE:
In a large saucepan, use a small amount of oil to sauté the bones. When the bones have a nice dark-brown color, remove them and add the tomato paste, mire poix, and bouquet garni. Drain off the oil. Put bones back in pan, add 2½ quarts of water, and cook for 1 hour to make stock. In another saucepan, add shallots, wine, and port and let the liquid reduce until it is almost gone. Add the stock to the wine reduction and cook for 40 minutes. Pass through a fine strainer, and add salt and pepper to taste.

FOR THE PRESENTATION:
Film a sauté pan with oil and sauté medallions (three per person) over medium heat to desired doneness. Heat the butter, add the apples and powdered sugar, and sauté the apples for 25 seconds on each side. Blanch the carrots and asparagus.

Place the medallions like three petals pointing out from the center of the plate. Between the outer edge of the medallions, place two slices of apple curving outward like wings. Between the arches of the apples, place one baby carrot between two asparagus tips. Sauce is placed over the medallions.

SERVES 6

Julian
Serrano

MEDALLONES DE VENADO CON MANZANAS VERDES CARAMELIZADAS

1 cuarto trasero de venado (55 gramos por medallón)

Aceite de oliva extra virgen

1 cucharada tomate en pasta

2 manojos mire poix (mezcla de cubitos de zanahoria, cebolla, apio y puerros)

Bouquet garni (mezcla de tomillo, hoja de laurel, perejil, puerro y apio en una bolsita hecha de gaza)

2 tazas vino tinto

2 cebollinos

½ taza vino oporto

Sal y pimienta

6 cucharadas mantequilla clarificada

5 manzanas Granny Smith (verdes, ácidas)

2 cucharadas azúcar glas

18 zanahorias pequeñitas

36 puntas de espárragos

Quite los huesos y limpie la carne. Guarde los trocitos de carne y los huesos para la salsa. Corte la carne en medallones. Corte los huesos en trozos pequeños.

PARA LA SALSA:

En una olla grande, use una pequeña cantidad de aceite para saltear los huesos. Asegúrese de dejarlos bien doraditos. Cuando los huesos obtengan un color marrón oscuro, saquélos y agregue el tomate en pasta, mire poix y bouquet garni. Quite el aceite. Ponga los huesos nuevamente en el sartén, agregue 2⅓ litros de agua y cocine por una hora. En otra olla, agregue los cebollinos, vino y oporto y deje que el líquido se reduzca hasta que casi se haya evaporado todo. Agregue el caldo a esta reducción y cocine por 40 minutos. Pase todo por un colador súper fino y agregue sal y pimienta al gusto.

PARA LA PRESENTACIÓN:

Saltée los medallones (3 por persona) a fuego medio hasta que estén hechos a su preferencia. Caliente la mantequilla, añada las manzanas y azúcar glas. Saltée las manzanas por 25 segundos por cada lado. Pase las zanahorias y los espárragos por agua caliente muy rápidamente.

Ponga los medallones como si fueran 3 pétalos apuntado hacia la parte exterior del plato. Entre las puntas exteriores de los medallones ponga dos trozos de manzana encurvándose hacia fuera como alas. Entre cada arco de manzanas, ponga una zanahoria dentro de dos puntas de espárrago. La salsa se pone sobre los medallones.

SIRVE 6

ARROZ CON GRANDULES

1½ tablespoon olive oil
1 tablespoon recaito (see below)
1 clove garlic, chopped
½ yellow onion, diced
½ cup tomato sauce

1 can Vienna sausage (may substitute diced ham)
4 cups rice
1 can (16 ounces) grandules (pigeon peas)
1½ cans (16 ounces) water

FOR THE RECAITO:
½ medium yellow onion, diced
2 cloves garlic, peeled
3 recao leaves (or triple amount of cilantro)

1 sprig cilantro

Put the olive oil in a large pot and heat over medium heat. Add the recaito, garlic, and onion, and sauté until onion is soft. Pour in the tomato sauce and stir. Cut up the sausage or ham, add to the pot, and cook until heated through. Add the rice and stir to let the flavors mingle. Add the can of grandules with 1½ cans of water. Let boil, uncovered. After you let it boil, reduce heat, cover, and simmer until rice is done.

SERVES 6

1½ cucharadas aceite de oliva
1 cuchara recaito (receta sigue)
1 diente de ajo
½ cebolla amarilla, cortada
½ taza salsa de tomate

1 lata chorizo de Vienna (o jamón cortado)
4 tazas arroz
1 lata grandules
1½ latas agua

PARA EL RECAITO:
½ cebolla amarilla, cortada
2 dientes de ajo, pelado
3 hojas de recao (o triple la cantidad de cilantro)

1 hoja cilantro

Poner el aceite de oliva en una cazuela sobre fuego mediano. Añadir recaito, ajo y cebolla y cocinar hasta que la cebolla este suave. Agregar la salsa de tomate y mezclar. Cortar el chorizo (o jamón) y cocinar. Añadir el arroz y dejar que los sabores se mezclen. Agregar los grandules con 1½ latas de agua. Dejar hervir, destapada. Despues de dejar hervir, bajar a fuego lento, tapar y cocinar hasta que el arroz esté cocido.

SIRVE 6

Rachel Ticotin

THIS DISH IS WHAT COMES TO MIND WHEN I THINK OF MY MOTHER. I HAVE SO MANY MEMORIES OF HER STANDING OVER A POT COOKING THIS. WE WOULD NEVER HAVE THOUGHT ABOUT EATING THIS AT A RESTAURANT. NOW, WITH THE HECTIC SCHEDULES WE ALL HAVE, WE'RE GRATEFUL TO FIND A PUERTO RICAN RESTAURANT ANYWHERE, BUT NOTHING CAN COMPARE WITH THE LOVE AND CARE INVESTED IN MY MOTHER'S COOKING.

Liz Torres

SOPA DE CREMA AGUACATE (COLD AVOCADO CREAM SOUP)

4 medium-sized ripe avocados (about 8 ounces each)

3 cans (13¾ ounces each) chicken broth

1 tablespoon lemon juice

2 cups light cream or half and half (1 pint)

1 tablespoon fresh or 1 teaspoon dried dill weed

1½ teaspoons salt

¼ teaspoon white pepper

Cut avocados in half. Remove pits and spoon pulp into a blender with about 1½ cans chicken broth and lemon juice. Blend on medium speed, stopping and stirring frequently with a rubber spatula, until smooth.

Pour avocado puree into a large glass bowl or soup tureen. Stir in the remaining chicken broth, light cream or half and half, dill, salt, and pepper. Cover bowl with plastic wrap. Chill. Garnish with fresh dill or chives, if desired.

SERVES 4

---

4 aguacates maduros

3 latas caldo de pollo

1 cucharada jugo de limón

2 tazas crema lijera

1 cucharada eneldo

1½ cucharitas sal

¼ cucharita pimienta blanca

Cortar los aguacates por la mitad. Remover la semilla, poner la pulpa en una batidora con 1½ latas de caldo de pollo y jugo de limón. Batir, parando de vez en cuando para mezclar con una cuchara, hasta que tenga una consistencia de sopa.

Poner el puré en una cazuela honda. Mezclar con el caldo de pollo que queda, crema lijera, eneldo, sal y pimienta. Tapar con papel plástico y enfriar en la nevera. Adornar con eneldo fresco.

SIRVE 4

MAYTAG BLUE AND PEAR SALAD, AGED SHERRY VINAIGRETTE

1 ounce aged sherry wine vinegar
4 ounces fruity, low-acid extra virgin olive oil
Coarse salt and freshly cracked black
   pepper to taste

6 ounces fresh mixed greens
3 fully ripened pears
6 ounces Maytag blue cheese

FOR THE AGED SHERRY VINAIGRETTE:

Combine the vinegar, oil, salt, and pepper and shake well in a covered jar (to prevent the vinegar's fragile fragrance esters from escaping). Taste and adjust for salt and pepper. (If too acidic for your taste, add a scant teaspoon of honey.) Cover jar and set aside for flavors to marry.

PREPARING THE MIXED GREENS:

To assure crisp, dry greens, rinse them in a cold-water bath. Lift greens from water into a colander. After draining, shake off remaining water in a salad spinner. Spread greens out on a kitchen towel, cover with another towel, and refrigerate in a closed container or plastic bag.

ASSEMBLING THE SALAD:

Bring cheese to room temperature (about 30 minutes). Halve the pears, remove cores, and place them flesh down on a cutting board. Slice in the strips. Toss them in the vinaigrette and set aside while you toss the greens in the dressing. Mound the greens in the center of six room-temperature plates. Sprinkle them lightly with coarse salt and pepper. Season the dressed pear strips with salt and pepper. Arrange them around the greens. Garnish the salads with crumbles of the blue cheese.

SERVES 6

Lance Dean Velasquez

LANCE DEAN VELASQUEZ, PARTNER/OWNER AND CHEF OF EPICENTER, IS HAPPY TO BE BACK IN SAN FRANCISCO AFTER BEING CHEF DE CUISINE OF HERITAGE HOUSE WHEN IT REOPENED FOR THE SEASON ON FEBRUARY 14, 1997. HE HAS BUILT HIS PROFESSIONAL CREDENTIALS AT SOME OF NORTHERN CALIFORNIA'S BEST ESTABLISHMENTS.

A NATIVE OF CALIFORNIA'S SONOMA VALLEY WINE COUNTRY, HIS COOKING CAREER BEGAN AT THE AGE OF 13, IN HIS MOTHER'S SANTA ROSA CAFÉ. HE WORKED HIS WAY TO SONOMA VALLEY'S CHATEAU SOUVERAIN, WHERE HE BECAME SOUS CHEF TO GARY DANKO, WHO ENCOURAGED HIM TO EARN A CULINARY, HOTEL, AND RESTAURANT MANAGEMENT DEGREE.

DURING HIS STUDENT YEARS IN SAN FRANCISCO, LANCE WORKED IN SEVERAL PRESTIGIOUS KITCHENS. AFTER GRADUATION, HE RETURNED TO HIS ROLE AS SOUS CHEF TO DANKO. THIS

Lance Dean Velasquez

TIME AT THE RESTAURANT AT THE RITZ CARLTON. CHEF JAN BIRNBAUM RECRUITED HIM FOR CAMPTON PLACE, WHERE HE WAS EVENTUALLY DISCOVERED BY ED AND MARY ETTA MOOSE.

AS FOUNDING CHEF OF SAN FRANCISCO'S HIGHLY SUCCESSFUL MOOSE'S, LANCE'S ACCLAIMED FOOD MADE HIM ONE OF THE NATION'S CULINARY RISING STARS, TOPPING CRITIC JOHN MARIANI'S LIST OF NINE "RISING STAR CHEFS" IN THE NOVEMBER 1993 ISSUE OF *ESQUIRE* MAGAZINE.

AN OFFER OF EQUAL PARTNERSHIP LED HIM TO BERKELEY, CALIFORNIA, WHERE HE FOUNDED THE EPONYMOUSLY NAMED RESTAURANT LDV. HIS CONTEMPORARY AMERICAN CUISINE QUICKLY BUILT A STRONG CORE OF FOLLOWERS, AND EARNED HIGH CRITICAL ACCLAIM. MICHAEL BAUER OF THE *SAN FRANCISCO CHRONICLE* NAMED LANCE "RISING STAR CHEF" IN 1995. WHEN THE PARTNERSHIP PROVED EPHEMERAL, LANCE MOVED TO ATLANTA FOR A STINT AT 1848 HOUSE IN MARIETTA, GA., WHERE HE SIGNED ON AS EXECUTIVE CHEF TO TAKE THE LANDMARK PLANTATION RESTAURANT THROUGH THE BALLOONING BUSINESS OF THE 1996 OLYMPICS. WHILE AT 1848 HOUSE, HE WAS VOTED ONE OF THE 10 BEST NEW AMERICAN CHEFS BY *FOOD & WINE* MAGAZINE.

ENSALADA DE QUESO AZUL MAYTAG CON VINAGRETA DE JEREZ AÑEJO

28 gramos vinagre de jerez añejo
112 gramos aceite de oliva extra virgen, afrutado y bajo en acidez
Sal y pimienta recién molida, al gusto

168 gramos verduras mixtas frescas
3 peras bien maduras
168 gramos queso azul Maytag

PARA LA VINAGRETA DE JEREZ AÑEJO:
Combine el vinagre, aceite, sal y pimienta y agite bien en un frasco cubierto (para prevenir que la fragancia delicada del vinagre se escape). Pruébelo y añada más sal y pimienta si lo necesita. (Si es muy ácido para su gusto, agregue un poquito de miel.) Cubra el frasco y póngalo a un lado para que se mezclen los sabores.

PREPARACIÓN DE LAS VERDURAS MIXTAS:
Para obtener verduras crujientes y secas, enjuáguelas en un baño de agua fría. Saque las verduras del agua y póngalas en un colador. Después de dejarlas reposar, sacuda el agua restante en un girador de ensaladas. Esparza las verduras en una toalla de cocina, cúbralas con otra toalla y refrigere en un recipiente cerrado o en una bolsa de plástico.

PREPARACIÓN DE LA ENSALADA:
Deje que el queso obtenga una temperatura ambiental (unos 30 minutos). Parta las peras a la mitad, quite los corazones y póngalas con la piel hacia arriba en una tablita para cortar. Córtelas en tiras. Revuélvalas en la vinagreta y póngalas a un lado mientras usted revuelve las verduras en el aderezo. Ponga las verduras en un montoncito al centro de seis platos a temperatura ambiental. Espolvoree ligeramente sal y pimienta. Sazone las tiras de pera con sal y pimienta. Arréglelas alrededor de las verduras. Decore las ensaladas con moronas de queso azul.

SIRVE 6

GREEN APPLE GRATIN WITH WARM NUTMEG CREAM

FOR THE NUTMEG CREAM:

2 cups heavy cream
¼ cup butter
¼ teaspoon freshly ground nutmeg
½ cup sugar
¼ teaspoon salt

Combine all ingredients in a heavy-bottomed saucepan and bring to a simmer. Simmer over low heat, whisking occasionally, until reduced to 2½ cups. Transfer to food processor (or blender) and pulse until texture is smooth.

FOR THE STREUSEL:

¾ cup plus 2 teaspoons all-purpose flour
¾ cup sugar
¾ teaspoon ground cinnamon
⅛ teaspoon salt
3 tablespoons cold butter

While nutmeg cream sauce is reducing, put flour, sugar, cinnamon, and salt into mixer bowl and mix with the paddle attachment until combined. Add butter and blend until like fine sand.

FOR SPICE MIX AND APPLES:

¼ cup sugar
½ teaspoon ground cinnamon
½ teaspoon ground nutmeg
⅛ teaspoon ground cloves
⅛ teaspoon salt
6 tart green apples (Pippin or Granny Smith)

Combine spices. Cut apples into quarters, peel, remove cores, and slice lengthwise. Toss apple slices with the spice mix. Arrange a single layer of apple slices in six buttered gratin dishes. Pour 1 tablespoon nutmeg cream over each, and top with ¼ inch of streusel. Bake at 350 degrees until apples are soft and streusel is golden. Serve warm with a scoop of vanilla ice cream and 2 ounces of the warm nutmeg cream.

SERVES 6

Lance Dean
Velasquez

GRATINADO DE MANZANA VERDE Y CREMA TEMPLADA DE NUEZ MOSCADA

PARA LA CREMA DE NUEZ MOSCADA:

2 tazas crema para batir (nata lìquida)
1/4 taza mantequilla
1/4 cucharita nuez moscada fresca, en polvo
1/2 taza azúcar
1/4 cucharadita sal

Combine todos los ingredientes en una olla gruesa y deje que hierva. Déjelo hervir a fuego lento, moviendo ocasionalmente, hasta que se haya reducido a 2 1/2 tazas. Pase todo al procesador de alimentos (o a la batidora) y pulse hasta que la textura sea lisa.

PARA EL ADEREZO:

3/4 taza más 2 cucharitas harina
3/4 taza azúcar
3/4 cucharita canela
1/8 cucharita sal
3 cucharadas mantequilla fría

Mientras se está reduciendo la salsa de crema de nuez moscada, ponga todos los ingredientes secos en el recipiente de la batidora y mezcle con el accesorio de paleta que viene con su mezclador. Añada la mantequilla y mezcle todo hasta que quede como arena fina.

PARA LA MEZCLA DE ESPECIAS Y MANZANAS, PREPARAR, HORNEAR Y SERVIR:

1/4 taza azúcar
1/2 cucharita canela
1/2 cucharita nuez moscada
1/8 cucharita clavos molidos
1/8 cucharita sal
6 manzanas verdes agrias (Pippin o Granny Smith)

Combine las especias. Corte las manzanas en cuartos, pélelas, quite los corazones y rebánelas a lo largo. Mezcle las rebanadas de manzana con la mezcla de especias. Arregle una capa de rebanadas de manzana en 6 platos para gratinar, previamente engrasados. Ponga 1 cucharada de crema sobre cada uno y ponga 1/2 centímetro del aderezo. Hornee a 350 grados F hasta que las manzanas estén blandas y el aderezo esté dorado. Sirva caliente con una bola de helado de vainilla y 55 gramos de la crema de nuez moscada caliente.

SIRVE 6

CARNE MECHADA

4 tablespoons olive oil
1 medium onion, diced
1 medium green bell pepper, diced
1 medium red bell pepper, diced
½ pound cooked ham steak, diced
½ cup alcaparado (olive salad), diced
Salt to taste
Black pepper to taste

Adobo seasoning
1 (6- to 10-pound) beef roast
1 packet Sazon brand seasoning
2½ pounds potatoes, peeled
1 pound carrots
1 packet or cube Goya beef stock
2 cups water

Lauren Velez

THIS IS ONE OF MY SISTER JOAQUINA'S FAVORITE RECIPES. SHE PASSED IT ON TO ME, SO I AM PASSING IT ON TO YOU *CON AMOR*. I HOPE YOU ENJOY IT AS MUCH AS MY *FAMILIA* DOES.

In a caldero (small cauldron) over medium heat, add 2 tablespoons of olive oil and the diced onion, green bell pepper, red bell pepper, ham steak, and alcaparado. Sauté and season to taste with salt, pepper, and adobo seasoning. Remove from caldero and set aside.

Rinse and dry the roast. With a boning knife, cut a pocket along the side almost all the way through the roast to make a cavity. Stuff with sautéed mixture. With a 1½-yard section of twine, tie the roast closed so the ingredients don't spill out. Rub Sazon seasoning all over the roast. Heat remaining 2 tablespoons of olive oil in caldero and brown roast on all sides.

While meat is browning, preheat oven to 450 degrees, cut the potatoes in quarters, and cut the carrots into ½-inch pieces. In a roasting pan, add 1½ cups of water, packet or cube of beef stock, potatoes, carrots, and the roast.

Roast everything for 1½ to 2 hours, checking every half hour and basting frequently. Once done, remove meat from the roasting pan. Let cool for 10 to 15 minutes. Cut twine and slice meat. Put on a platter, garnish with potatoes and carrots, and dress with gravy drippings from pan.

---

4 cucharadas aceite de oliva
1 cebolla mediana, cortada
1 ají verde, cortado
1 ají rojo, cortado
227 gramos jamón cocido, cortado
½ taza alcaparado
Sal (al gusto)
Pimienta (al gusto)

Adobo sazón
1 rosbif (3 a 4½ kilogramos)
1 paquete Sazón
1 kilogramo papas, peladas
454 gramos zanahoria
1 paquete caldo de carne Goya
2 tazas agua

En un caldero sobre fuego mediano, agregar 2 cucharadas de aceite de oliva y cebollas cortadas, ajíes verdes y rojos, jamón y alcaparado. Cocer y sazonar a gusto con sal, pimienta y adobo. Remover del caldero y poner a un lado.

Lavar y secar el rosbif. Con un cuchillo, cortar un hoyo contra un lado de la carne para hacer una cavidad. Rellenar con la mezcla. Con un cordel, cieralo para que los ingredientes no se salgan. Sazonar la carne con el paquete de Sazón. Calentar 2 cucharadas de aceite de oliva en el caldero y cocer la carne hasta que pierda el color.

En lo que se esté cocinando, poner el horno 450 grados y cortar las papas peladas y zanahoria. En una cazuela añadir 1½ tazas de agua, caldo de carne, papas, zanahorias y la carne.

Asar todo por 1½ a 2 horas. Cuando esté cocido, remover del horno. Dejar enfríar por 10 a 15 minutos. Cortar el cordel y cortar la carne. Poner en un plato de servir, adornar con papas y zanahorias y con la salsa de la carne.

Daphne Zuniga

MAMA PITY'S TAMALES

FOR THE MEAT:

3 pounds pork butt or 1 (3-pound) chicken   1 head garlic

In a large pot, put pork butt or chicken with head of garlic and water to cover. Bring to a boil, skim off scum, and let simmer for 1 hour until meat is fall-off-the-bone tender. Remove pot from heat and let cool. Once cool, reserve the liquid to mix with masa and shred meat into strips to use later in tamales.

FOR THE RECADO:

15 tomatoes	1 small stick of cinnamon
2 chilies guaques rojas	4 French bread rolls
2 chilies pimientos	4 ounces sesame seeds
1 large onion	4 ounces pepitoria
3 cloves garlic	Achiote or tomato paste

Toast the tomatoes, chilies, onion, and garlic in a baking pan in the oven at 350 degrees or on an ungreased griddle over medium-high heat until the vegetables blister and develop dark, roasted areas. Cool, transfer to blender or food processor, add cinnamon, and puree. Remove to mixing bowl. Soak the French rolls in water until they are soft and puree in blender or food processor. Add sesame seeds and pepitoria and blend. Then add bread puree mixture a bit at a time to thicken sauce, while adding achiote or tomato paste for color.

FOR THE MASA:

1 (2-pound) bag of Masa Harina or Maseca brands prepared corn masa	4 sticks margarine or 2 cups vegetable oil
16 cups water	Broth from pork or chicken

In a large mixing bowl, mix the prepared masa, water, and margarine or vegetable oil. If too thick, add broth for flavor. If too thin, add more recado until masa is firm but spreadable.

FOR THE TAMALES:

Banana leaves (amount depends on whether fresh or frozen)	Olives
	Canned chilies pimientos

To assemble tamales, spread 4 or 5 tablespoons of masa on a single banana leaf. Press down with a sheet of waxed paper to even masa. Once smooth, remove paper and then, down the center of the masa, spoon 2 heaping spoonfuls of the recado, then a piece or two of pork or chicken, followed by an olive and piece of the canned chili pimiento. Fold the two sides of the banana leaf first, then take a second leaf and fold it over the tamale, then fold the top and bottom parts over to create a secure package.

To cook the tamales, take the scraps of the banana leaves and bunch them in the bottom of a large steamer. Place tamales, as you assemble them, seam-side down on top of banana leaf scraps. Once full, fill with 2 to 3 inches of water, set over medium heat, and bring to a boil, then reduce to a simmer and let steam for an hour or until the tamales are done, which is when the masa is no longer soft and holds its shape.

SERVES 20

TAMALES DE MAMA PITY

PARA LA CARNE:

1½ kilogramos cerdo o pollo   1 cabeza ajo

En una caldera, poner el cerdo o pollo con la cabeza de ajo y agua y tapar. Poner a hervir y poner a fuego lento por una hora. Remover de la caldera y dejar enfríar. Cuando este frío, reservar el líquido para mezclar con la masa y cortar la carne para utilizar mas tarde.

PARA EL RECADO:

15 tomates	1 rama de canela
2 chiles guaques rojas	4 pedazos de pan Frances
2 chiles pimientos	100 gramos anjonjolí
1 cebolla grande	100 gramos pepitoria
3 dientes de ajo	Achiote o pasta de tomate

Tostar los tomates, chiles, cebollas y ajo en una cazuela en el horno a 350 grados hasta cocido. Enfríar, añadir canela y poner en una batidora. Poner en una cazuela para mezclar. Ponga el pan en agua hasta que este suave y poner a batir en una batidora. Añadir anjonjolí y pepitoria y batir. Añadir la mezcla de pan con achiote o la pasta de tomate.

PARA LA MASA:

1 kilogramo Masa Harina o harina de maíz maseca	2 tazas de aceite vegetal
16 tazas agua	Caldo de cerdo o pollo

En una cazuela, mezclar la masa, agua y aceite de vegetal. Añadir caldo hasta que la masa esté dura, pero manejable.

PARA LOS TAMALES:

Hojas de plátanos (la cantidad depende de si están frescas o congeladas)	Aceitunas
	Chiles pimientos de lata

Para hacer los tamales, poner 4 o 5 cucharadas de masa en una hoja de plátano, aplastar con papel encerado, para dividir la masa en la hoja. Remover el papel, en el centro de la masa poner 2 cucharadas del recado, luego uno o dos pedazos de pollo o cerdo, después una aceituna y un pedazo de chile pimiento. Doblar los lados de la hoja primero, luego los lados opuestos para asegurar el paquete.

Para cocinarlo, poner pedazos de las hojas de plátano en el fondo de una olla vaporera. Poner los tamales, encima. Cuando esté lleno, poner 5 a 7½ centímetros de agua y poner sobre fuego mediano y poner a hervir, bajar a fuego lento y dejar cocer al vapor por una hora o hasta que esté cocido, que es cuando la masa no esté blanda.

SIRVE 20

Daphne Zuniga

CONVERSION CHART

APPROXIMATE METRIC EQUIVALENTS BY WEIGHT

U.S.	Metric
1/4 ounce	7 grams
1/2 ounce	14 grams
1 ounce	28 grams
1 1/4 ounces	35 grams
1 1/2 ounces	40 grams
1 2/3 ounces	45 grams
2 ounces	55 grams
2 1/2 ounces	70 grams
4 ounces	112 grams
5 ounces	140 grams
8 ounces	228 grams
10 ounces	280 grams
15 ounces	425 grams
16 ounces (1 pound)	454 grams

Metric	U.S.
1 gram	.035 ounce
50 grams	1.75 ounces
100 grams	3.5 ounces
250 grams	8.75 ounces
500 grams	1.1 pounds
1 kilogram	2.2 pounds

APPROXIMATE METRIC CONVERSIONS BY VOLUME

U.S.	Metric
1 tablespoon	15 milliliters
1/4 cup	60 milliliters (0.56 deciliters)
1/3 cup	80 milliliters (0.75 deciliters)
1/2 cup	120 milliliters (1.13 deciliters)
2/3 cup	160 milliliters (1.5 deciliters)
1 cup	230 milliliters (2.27 deciliters)
1 1/4 cups	300 milliliters
1 1/2 cups	360 milliliters
1 2/3 cups	400 milliliters
2 cups	460 milliliters
2 1/2 cups	600 milliliters
3 cups	600 milliliters (6.81 deciliters)
4 cups (1 quart)	.95 liter
1.05 quarts	1 liter
4 quarts (1 gallon)	3.8 liters

Metric	U.S.
50 milliliters	.21 cup
100 milliliters	.42 cup
150 milliliters	.63 cup
200 milliliters	.84 cup
250 milliliters	1.06 cups
1 liter	1.05 quarts

APPROXIMATE METRIC EQUIVALENTS BY LENGTH

U.S.	Metric
1/8 inch	.3 centimeters
1/4 inch	.6 centimeters
1 inch	2.5 centimeters
2 inches	5.08 centimeters
4 inches	10.16 centimeters
5 inches	13 centimeters
6 inches	15.24 centimeters
8 inches	20.32 centimeters
9 inches	22.86 centimeters
10 inches	25.4 centimeters
12 inches	30.48 centimeters
14 inches	35.56 centimeters
16 inches	40.64 centimeters
20 inches	50.8 centimeters

APPROXIMATE OVEN TEMPERATURES

Fahrenheit	Celsius
250	120
300	150
325	160
350	180
375	190
400	200
425	220
450	230
475	240
500	260

INDEX

PHOTO CREDITS

All food photographs by Butch Monserrat. Other photo credits as follows:

10: Naomi Kaltman

11: James Tipton

14: Nacho Pinedo

15: Steven Gallagher

16: Marc Raboy

25: Leslie Sokolow

26: Casey Stoll

27: Randee St. Nicholas

32: Joe Gato

36: Kevin McGowen

40: Ricardo Betancourt

48: Eduardo MuEoz

63: Angela Cappetta

66: Linda Borgeson

67: Marco Micheletti

74: Timothy White (Courtesy of
   Paramount Pictures)

76: Charla Wood

82: Paul Gregory

85: Steven Lippman

86: Rory Ivers

88: David Hughes

92: Barry King

93: Jonathon Exley

101: Ron Rinaldi

104: Carlos Somonte

108: Rico Torres

109: Richard Reinsdorf

113: Patricia de la Rosa

128: Marc Raboy

131: Dennis Galante

135: Diego Robledo

137: Andrew Melick

147: Angela Cappetta

148: Carlos Carrera

153: Angela Cappetta